D1637486

FORM 125 M

The Chicago Public Library
BUSINESS/SCIENCE/TECHNOLOGY DIVISION

Received

FAMOUS REGIMENTS

The Duke of Wellington's Regiment

Lieutenant-Colonel The Hon. Arthur Wesley. Commanded 33rd Regiment 1793–1802. Colonel of the Regiment 1806–1813, later 1st Duke of Wellington

FAMOUS REGIMENTS

Edited by
Lt.-General Sir Brian Horrocks

The Duke of Wellington's Regiment (West Riding)

(The 33rd/76th Regiment of Foot)

by James Lunt

Leo Cooper Ltd., London

First published in Great Britain, 1971
by Leo Cooper Ltd
196 Shaftesbury Avenue, London W.C.2
Copyright © 1971 by James Lunt
Introduction Copyright © 1971 by
Lt.-General Sir Brian Horrocks

ISBN 0 85052 067 3

PRINTED IN GREAT BRITAIN
BY EBENEZER BAYLIS AND SON LTD.
THE TRINITY PRESS, WORCESTER, AND LONDON

The Duke of Wellington's Regiment
(West Riding)

A SPECIAL INTRODUCTION
by Lt.-General Sir Brian Horrocks

Whether or not the Battle of Waterloo was won on the playing-fields of Eton, there is no doubt that the last major defensive battle fought by British troops, namely the Battle of the Hook in Korea, as well as many other desperate actions in both world wars, was won by the regiment that proudly bears the Duke of Wellington's name on the Rugby Football grounds of the United Kingdom. As young officers we cynically said that to get a commission in the Dukes one had either to have a close family connection or to have played for the Royal Military College at Rugby Football; I expect this was because we were always beaten by them. For one regiment to have won the Army Rugby Cup nine times and to have been runners-up twice is a truly remarkable achievement. Anyone who has been a soldier will know what a profound effect such a record has on the morale of a regiment, and it is morale which wins battles.

In the course of this series I have read the histories of many famous regiments, but after I had read General Lunt's Prologue I felt that there was nothing more I could possibly add. I found it very moving indeed, because the 33rd and 76th Foot, who in 1881 were combined to form the First and Second Battalions, The Duke of Wellington's Regiment, contain all those qualities which made the best British county regiments what they were. Above all, they were one family belonging to the West Riding, where, in the author's words 'the climate is rugged, the men are tough, independent in mind, slow to anger but as hard as nails'—the perfect infantryman in fact; but as he goes on to say, 'easy to lead but devils to drive'.

In its early days the Regiment was spared none of the trials and tribulations of military service and one or other battalion seems to have played a distinguished role in almost every major campaign fought by the British Army. Their regimental day is, of course, the anniversary of Waterloo, where the 33rd took part in that memorable charge which routed Napoleon's Imperial Guard and so altered the face of Europe.

For me to say more is superfluous, so brilliantly has General Lunt discharged his duty; but there is one chapter to which I would like to draw special attention. It is the chapter entitled 'Hindoostan' and it is a very remarkable account of the operations carried out by the 76th Foot during their 18 years in India. I happen to be one of those very rare birds of my generation, a regular army officer who never served in India, so much of General Lunt's account is new to me. The hardships which the troops suffered, owing to totally inadequate administrative resources and a complete absence of medical facilities, are almost beyond belief. It is hardly surprising that when the Regiment sailed for home in February, 1806, only two men remained who had embarked at Gravesend in 1787.

I am sure that all who read this book will join me in congratulating General Lunt on producing a history of which the West Riding of Yorkshire can justly be proud.

Acknowledgements

It is a daunting requirement to compress the history of a famous regiment into a book of this size; it is not so much a case of what to include as what to leave out, and no two people are likely to agree on the relative importance of this or that episode in a regiment's history. I am acutely aware of the imperfections of this short history of the Duke of Wellington's Regiment and I regret it the more because I consider it a great honour to have been invited to write this book. I began my military career in the Dukes thirty-three years ago, and although our paths have since diverged nothing can diminish my affection for the Regiment nor my pride in its splendid record and traditions. For this reason I wish it had proved possible to deal more adequately with the mass of material placed at my disposal.

The Regiment is fortunate in possessing excellent records of its past, of which by far the best source is the regimental magazine, *The Iron Duke*. There are also—*The History of the 33rd* by Albert Lee; *Historical Records of the 76th 'Hindoostan' Regiment 1787–1881* by Lt-Colonel F. A. Hayden; *History of the Duke of Wellington's Regiment 1881–1923* by Brig-General C. D. Bruce; and the *History of the Duke of Wellington's Regiment 1919–52* by Brigadier C. N. Barclay; and several excellent recruiting pamphlets. All this material has been placed at my disposal and I must place on record my appreciation for the help I have been given by Major John Davis, Regimental Secretary at Regimental Headquarters in Halifax, and Major Tony Savory who has contributed many interesting articles on regimental history in *The Iron Duke*; we were subalterns together in the 2nd

Battalion in India—longer ago than I care to remember!—
and I have welcomed this opportunity to rekindle old
friendships. Brigadier B. W. Webb-Carter, who commanded
the 33rd with great distinction in North Africa and Italy,
and who is Chairman of the Council of the Society of Army
Historical Research, has also been of great assistance. I have
been fortunate in having been able to write this book while
serving at Supreme Headquarters Allied Powers Europe
at a time when General Sir Robert Bray, Colonel of the
Regiment, has been Deputy Supreme Commander. I am
most grateful for the interest he has shown in this book and
for his advice and criticism. And finally I must thank my
excellent stenographer, Corporal William Davis, R.A.F.,
for the time and effort he has devoted to typing the manu-
script.

Mons, Belgium   J.D.L.
                                                March, 1970

Prologue

THIS IS the story of an English county regiment which can justifiably claim, along with its sister-regiments, to be the backbone of the British Army. That this is no idle boast is supported by no less an individual than the Duke of Wellington himself, in conversation with Mr Creevey just before the Battle of Waterloo.

Mr Creevey 'Will you let me ask you, Duke, what you think you will make of it?'
The Duke 'By God! I think Blücher and myself can do the thing.'
Mr Creevey 'Do you calculate upon any desertion in Buonaparte's army?'
The Duke 'Not upon a man, from the Colonel to the private in a regiment—both inclusive. We may pick up a Marshal or two, perhaps, but not worth a damn.'

Then Mr Creevey asked him about the French Royalists in Belgium.

'Oh!' said the Duke, 'don't mention such fellows! No: I think Blücher and I can do the business.'

At that moment his eye was caught by a British private in the green alleys of the Park; and as he watched the little scarlet figure staring at the foreign statues under the foreign trees,

'There,' said the Duke, pointing a long forefinger, 'It all depends upon that article whether we do the business or not. Give me enough of it and I am sure.'*

* *The Creevey Papers* 1903 Ch. X p. 228.

This was high praise from a man as sparing in praise as the Duke of Wellington, who on occasions had been far from complimentary about the British soldier. It would be tempting to believe that the private he pointed out to Mr Creevey belonged to the 33rd Foot, the regiment Wellington had joined as Arthur Wesley on April 30, 1793, and which at that moment was billeted in Soignies, not far from Brussels. Wellington had been a young and inexperienced major when he joined the 33rd, and it was in the 33rd that he learned his trade as a soldier, remaining on the regimental list until 1802, when he was promoted Major-General. Unfortunately, Mr Creevey did not bother to record the private's regiment, and not even in the history of the British Army, where legend is so often mixed up with tradition, is there any suggestion that the private came from the 33rd.

The Duke of Wellington's Regiment was named after the Duke nine months after his death and on the thirty-eighth anniversary of his greatest victory. The Regiment therefore enjoys 'the peculiar distinction of being the only British regiment named after a subject—not Royal.' This unique distinction was conferred on the 33rd Foot by Queen Victoria on June 18, 1853, and 28 years later was shared by the 76th Foot when, on July 4, 1881, that regiment was joined with the 33rd Foot to become the 2nd Battalion the Duke of Wellington's Regiment.

The Regiment's subsidiary title is the West Riding Regiment. For those who know the Dukes there is something about them that epitomizes the West Riding of Yorkshire, the home of solid, undemonstrative, but utterly dependable people, such as Jess Oakroyd, immortalized in J. B. Priestley's *Good Companions*. The West Riding is a land of contrasts, ranging from the factory-filled valleys to the wild, sweeping moors. Here the climate is rugged, and the men are tough, independent in mind, slow to anger, but as hard as nails. They work hard and they play hard, and they make some of the finest soldiers in the world—'easy to lead but devils to drive,' as my first company commander told me when I joined the regimental depot in Halifax in September, 1937.

They are not flamboyant folk, the men and women of the West Riding, and they prefer those with a no-nonsense, down-to-earth approach to life. The same can be said of their regiment, since the Dukes' attitude towards soldiering has always been the simple one of getting down to the job with the maximum effectiveness and the minimum fuss and noise. I remember asking a wounded soldier of the Dukes in hospital with me in Burma what he was hoping would happen to him. 'Gettin' out of this bloody hole and gettin' back t' lads!' he replied.

The story of a regiment is the story of men of similar spirit who throughout the years have done their duty as they saw it, without fuss, without acclaim, and without any expectation of reward. Some may have become generals, others R.S.M.s, but these have been the lucky ones. For the vast majority the sole reward has been the knowledge that they belonged to a good regiment which was at its best when the going was toughest; and although the Dukes would be the last to claim that they are in any way unique in this respect, they can equally claim that the cap fits and that therefore they are entitled to wear it.

It was Field-Marshal Slim, that great 'soldier's general', who wrote that the British soldier is not braver than other soldiers, but that he is brave for a bit longer. The Dukes needed that endurance when they served under him during the long retreat from Burma in 1942, and again in the fighting around Imphal in 1944. They needed it, too, at Anzio. They needed it when they were compelled to surrender after fighting against heavy odds at Almanza in Spain in 1707, and again at Yorktown in Virginia in 1781. They needed it at Seringapatam, Ally Ghur, and Bhurtpore in India, at the Alma and Inkerman in the Crimea, and perhaps above all in the bloody battles around Ypres in Flanders during the Great War. They needed it most recently at 'The Hook' in Korea, where they stood firm against everything the Communist Chinese could bring against them.

Morale, Field-Marshal Montgomery has written, is a pearl beyond price. In part it comes from the tradition of a good regiment, in part from many other sources. No-one has yet been able to decide the exact proportion of the ingredients that go towards the making of high morale, but one thing is certain. Yorkshire character, and the tradition inherited from more than two hundred years of soldiering, have combined to make the Dukes the first-class infantry regiment that it is today.

Chapter

I

The Beginning

THE DUKE of Wellington's Regiment can trace their descent—unbroken for almost 270 years—from a letter addressed to the Earl of Huntingdon and dated March 14, 1702. Huntingdon, then aged twenty-five and a lieutenant-colonel in the First Regiment of Foot Guards, was ordered in this letter to raise, 'by Beat of Drum or otherwise', a regiment of Foot for service in the war about to break out between Britain and France. The men were, preferably, to be volunteers, but few were forthcoming. Huntingdon was therefore forced to offer each man £3 for the privilege of serving his country, doubtless recouping himself later when he submitted the muster rolls to the Paymaster. He succeeded by hook or by crook in persuading some 700 men, mostly from the Midlands, to enlist; and then proceeded to billet them around Hereford and Gloucester on the unwilling inn-keepers, farmers and householders, who almost certainly considered soldiers to be little better than convicts. In those days, and for many years afterwards, the life of the soldier was hard, brutish, and frequently short, while his standing in the community was not calculated to attract any but the unemployed or unemployable.

Huntingdon's Regiment eventually found its way, after various vicissitudes, to Spain. Huntingdon did not accompany it, a regiment being more or less the property of its colonel, and it was Lieutenant-Colonel Duncanson who took the Regiment to war and who lost his life leading it at the storming of Valencia in 1705. Three years later, after much marching, counter-marching, and skirmishing with both the French and Spaniards, the Regiment was cut to pieces at Almanza on April 25, 1709, and was forced, with four other English regiments and a Dutch contingent, to surrender to greatly superior forces commanded by the Duke of Berwick. The Regiment had greatly distinguished itself at the storming of Valencia and it only surrendered at Almanza after all the ammunition was expended; it was later re-formed, only to be forced once again to surrender at Brigheuga in December, 1710. After the Treaty of Utrecht in 1711 the remnants of the Regiment were shipped to Ireland, where they were subsequently threatened with disbandment, but were saved from the axe by the Jacobite Rebellion in 1715. The Regiment has ever since enjoyed a continuous existence.

It used to be the practice in the British Army for regiments to bear the name of their colonel, and since colonels were constantly changing, for one reason or another, the names of regiments also changed at frequent intervals. Thus Huntingdon handed on the colonelcy to Duncanson, and he in turn was succeeded by Wade, later a Field-Marshal, who became notorious for the methods he adopted to pacify the Highlands after the Jacobite Rebellion of 1745; his road-building activities to open up the Highlands were beneficial in the long run but were offset by his ruthless proscription of the clans, which left long and bitter memories. Hawley succeeded Wade, and there were others to follow, such as Johnson, from whom the regiment was nicknamed 'Johnson's Jolly Dogs', but it would be confusing for the reader to keep changing the name of the regiment. Some uniformity was introduced into the army in 1751 when regiments were numbered, and the regiment became the 33rd Regiment of Foot. It will be referred to as such from here onwards, although this is not historically accurate.

*   *   *

The 33rd returned from Spain in 1711 and were not again involved in a campaign until 1743, when they embarked for Flanders to join the army assembling under the Earl of Stair for war against the French. This was the War of the Austrian Succession and even the military historian finds it difficult to chart his course through what has been described as 'the diffuse and muddled conflict between 1741 and 1748'.* So far as the British were concerned, the war was fought mostly in Flanders and Germany, where the unfortunate inhabitants were forced to endure active operations during the spring and summer, and the compulsory billeting of troops in their dwellings during the 'close season' of autumn and winter. War was conducted in almost formalized fashion, like the steps in the minuet, and in accordance with elaborate rules; for the ordinary foot soldier it was mostly a case of marching backwards and forwards across Flanders and Germany, with the occasional battle, siege or skirmish to break the monotony. Officers came and went, usually as the fancy took them, but the soldiers marched and fought until they were killed, died, were invalided out on account of wounds, or could march no more because they were too old. It was during one of these formalized manœuvres that the British, under King George II—the last occasion when a British monarch commanded in battle—were brought to battle on the banks of the river Main in Germany by the French under Noailles and Grammont. The battle of Dettingen followed on June 27, 1743 and the 33rd were in the thick of the fight, losing more officers than any other regiment. The staunchness of the British infantry checked the French cavalry and Dettingen was a victory. It is the Regiment's first battle honour.

Two years later the French under Saxe, the foremost soldier of his age, made a determined attempt to capture the important frontier fortress of Tournai. The allies—British, Germans and Dutch—under the king's son, the Duke of

* *Maria Theresa* by Edward Crankshaw (Longmans 1969).

Cumberland, hastened to the relief of the fortress. The French army was stronger and well-posted around the village of Fontenoy, but Cumberland was determined to attack. At 2 p.m. on May 11, 1745 the battle began. The 33rd formed part of the Allied centre and had to attack uphill, advancing steadily with shouldered arms for nearly a mile until they reached the French entrenchments, and being subjected throughout the advance to a hail of artillery fire. The British held their fire until they were within 30 yards of the French line when they halted—'two battalions loading while the third fired'. The French infantry and cavalry were shattered by this disciplined musketry and their entrenchments were charged, but, unfortunately, elsewhere on the field the allies failed to capture a key redoubt and the village of Fontenoy. Cumberland was therefore compelled to order a withdrawal, which was carried out as steadily as the advance, and although Fontenoy cannot be described as a victory, it was hardly a defeat. The British infantry have never acquitted themselves better and the 33rd left behind on the battlefield their Lieutenant-Colonel, Clements, four other officers and 42 rank and file.

They were recalled to England in September, 1745 on account of the Jacobite Rebellion, being sent to Scotland early in 1746. They did not take part in the battle of Culloden, but were employed in stamping out the embers of the rebellion, a not-particularly glorious episode in British history. Back in Flanders again before the end of the year, they took part in the battles of Roncoux and Lauffeld (the latter a near-disaster) before the war was ended by the Treaty of Aix-la-Chapelle in October, 1748. It had not been one of the best-conducted wars in British history, but the 33rd had fought bravely. For all the monotony of their existence and their squalid living-conditions, those simple Englishmen made excellent soldiers. They were easy to discipline, brave in attack, and staunch in defence. Perhaps their outstanding characteristic was the handling of their weapons, crude and cumbersome though these were, and it was during those early years of its existence that the British infantry first began to pride itself on its fire discipline, which was later to win it victory on many a stricken field. The 'Corporal Trims' of those days knew no other home than their regiments, which they regarded with a jealous pride, and could look for little attention to their welfare by their officers. Medical attention for the sick and wounded was virtually non-existent, bleeding or amputation being the sovereign remedies, and English poorhouses held more than their fair quota of limbless ex-soldiers living on the parish in return for the mutilation they had suffered in the service of their country. Many of them took wives, temporary or permanent, in the countries where they were serving, while others were followed to war by their own women who cared for them while in billets, and who scoured the battlefield for the wounded when the fighting was over—sometimes even while it was still continuing. We owe a great debt to those nameless soldiers who laid the foundations of the tradition we have inherited and whose graves were seldom marked with a headstone. Their only memorial is the Duke of Wellington's Regiment as it exists today.

★   ★   ★

As always, there was a rush to dismember the army as soon as the war was over. The 33rd escaped disbandment but were always short of men during the years of monotonous garrison duty that followed their return from Flanders. Similarly, there was again the usual last-minute rush to increase the strength of the army when war began to threaten with France in 1756. The 33rd, as a result of this war fever, acquired a second battalion in 1758, but it was renumbered the 72nd Foot shortly afterwards and disbanded five years later. Meanwhile the 33rd were involved in the abortive attacks on St Malo and Cherbourg, under the third Duke of Marlborough, who clearly had not inherited any of the military genius of his illustrious ancestor. A second attempt at Cherbourg, under a different commander, succeeded, but St Malo resisted capture and the embarkation was a disastrous episode, in the course of which the 33rd's Grenadier Company was all but annihilated.

The Seven Years' War is chiefly memorable in British history for the winning of a great empire overseas while the French were preoccupied in Europe, and the brunt of the fighting on the Continent was carried out by Britain's allies, Frederick the Great of Prussia and other German princes. But the King of England was also King of Hanover, with great German possessions, and the British could at no time afford to allow the French to seize Hanover. There were, therefore, British troops involved in operations on the Continent, and in 1760 these were considerably augmented by what the Duke of Newcastle, the then Prime Minister, described as 'The Glorious Reinforcement'. The 33rd formed part of this reinforcement, leaving England in May 1760 to join the forces operating in northern Germany under Prince Ferdinand of Brunswick.

It was about this time that a young man called Collins joined the 33rd as a volunteer and was appointed Ensign as a result of his mother's entreaties. Viscount Barrington was the Secretary at War and he wrote as follows to the Marquis of Granby, then commanding in Germany.

> I am told there is a vacancy of Lieutenant or Ensign in the 33rd Regiment, and that a young man of sixteen, son to Captn Collins of that corps, now actually carrys [sic] arms in it. If you had seen his mother, who is one of the handsomest women I ever beheld, and who does not seem above twenty herself, you would not have been able to refuse writing at her request such a letter as I now write . . . Do not let Mrs. Collin's reputation suffer by unjust suspicion. I never saw her but for one minute in my life, and probably shall never see her again.*

* Rutland Papers, ii. p. 354.

It is not surprising that young Collins got his ensigncy and the family had a long connection with not only the 33rd, but also with the 76th. They later changed their name to Dansey.

Ferdinand of Brunswick was an able soldier, and there was much fighting in defence of Hanover. The 33rd added to their reputation at Warburg, where their Grenadiers suffered heavy losses, and in numerous other engagements fought mostly in Westphalia. The Grenadier Company again distinguished itself at Wilhelmstahl, though by then the war was drawing to a close, due as much to the mutual exhaustion of the contestants as to any conclusive victory. Although the 33rd had missed being present at such decisive British victories as Plassey and Quebec they had played a worthy part in defending Hanover, and returned to England in 1763 with an excellent reputation.

After the Treaty of Fontainebleau, which ended the Seven Years' War, there was the usual scamper to reduce the strength of the army. The 33rd was drastically reduced in numbers and then endured the monotony of garrison life in England (where the army constituted more an armed constabulary than anything else); and the not much less monotonous life of an overseas garrison in Minorca. Supplies were in the hands of fraudulent contractors who made fortunes at the expense of the troops, and a regiment might remain overseas for 25 years or more without relief. Duties consisted mainly of drill and sentry-go, occasionally enlivened by brushes with smugglers or the suppression of a slave rebellion or similar uprising, while heavy drinking occupied most of the leisure hours. Service in Ireland was little better, as the 33rd were to discover when they were sent to Cork in 1770, since their function was very much that of an army of occupation. They were split up in small detachments all over the countryside and their accommodation was, if anything, even worse than it was in England. However, it was in Ireland that the 33rd received Earl Cornwallis to command them; they were to find him not only a good colonel but also a much better soldier than his subsequent fate in North America might suggest.

Trouble had been brewing with the North American Colonies ever since Grenville's unfortunate Stamp Act of 1765. It was probably inevitable that the colonists would sooner or later seek to sever themselves from the mother-country, but the short-sighted folly of the British government in picking a quarrel with them over that particular issue seems unbelievable today; however, subsequent British governments have made similar, if perhaps not quite so far-reaching, misjudgements, and there were as many 'wild men' and bigots in the Colonies as ever there were at Westminster. Once British troops had been attacked, as they were at Lexington on April 19, 1775, war became inevitable, and the usual hasty scratching-together of reinforcements began almost at once. Cornwallis's 33rd was one of the first to be called forward, notwithstanding the state of Ireland—itself on the verge of rebellion. Nine regiments were selected from the Irish garrison to reinforce the army in the North American colonies, and the 33rd was one of them; each contained twelve companies, with 56 effective rank and file in each company. The 33rd sailed from Cork on February 12, 1776 under the command of Lieutenant-Colonel Webster. Lord Cornwallis was in overall command of the force.

The 33rd sailed for America wearing, so far as the battalion companies were concerned, three-cornered hats, red coats and white waistcoats and breeches. They wore short black gaiters and the coats could be looped back to permit freer movement. The Grenadier Company was similarly dressed, but wore a fur cap instead of a three-cornered hat. A broad buff belt over the left shoulder supported a large leather pouch containing various articles of kit. A tin canteen and a plain canvas haversack also had to be accommodated, as well as the private's basket-hilted sword. The Light Company, added in 1771, wore short red jackets, red waistcoats, short gaiters and a leather cap; they carried a powder horn and bag. The principal weapon was the smoothbore firelock, later to be known as 'Brown Bess'; it weighed 9 pounds and fired a bullet sufficient to stop a charging elephant, but was inaccurate beyond 30 yards. It was basically an area weapon and was fired in volleys at short range; well-trained troops could load and fire three times in a minute. Sergeants carried swords and halberds, and officers espontoons, light pikes 7 feet long, in addition to their swords. However, these distinguishing marks were soon abandoned and both officers and sergeants were then armed with fusees. Contrary to the general idea, which believes the rebellious colonists to have been hawk-eyed sharpshooters, the majority of their troops were similarly equipped, and adopted much the same tactics, as the British. Since most of the colonists' generals had been trained in the British fashion, this is hardly surprising.

The regimental facings of the 33rd were scarlet and there was, of course, a profusion of lace of various kinds. Hair was worn long, usually tied behind in a pigtail, greased and powdered; and as if this was not sufficient to make turning the head difficult, a tight leather stock was also compulsory. Thus, trussed as securely as any fowl, laden like a pack-horse with camp kettle, blanket and tent poles, stiffened like automatons after years of drill, the 33rd set out to march their way round a country which was still more a primæval forest than anything else.

It took the 33rd three weary, storm-tossed months, months passed in appalling living-conditions, before they made their landfall at Charleston in South Carolina. They were shipped soon afterwards to New York and landed on Long Island on August 22, 1776. The American War of Independence is not one of the most glorious episodes in the history of the British Army, and the reason for this is not hard to see. The soldiers fought well enough, the officers were gallant, and there were some good generals. But the home government consistently under-estimated the colonists and the difficulties facing their own commanders. The insistence of the War Secretary, Lord George Germaine, in keeping all control in his own hands was not calculated to help, for, quite apart from Germaine's bad military record and obstinate character, it took weeks for despatches to travel backwards and forwards between New York and London. Nor were matters helped by the dilatory character of General Howe who commanded until 1778; it took Howe a long time to make up his mind and even longer to act on it. Clinton, who succeeded him, was little better, but Cornwallis, operating under Clinton, was regarded by the Americans as the best of the British generals.

The war can best be divided into two halves. In the first, the British concentrated on dealing with New England, the seat of the rebellion in the first place, and on bringing Washington to battle and destroying him. They very nearly succeeded in the latter on several occasions, and the 33rd were involved in several fierce actions, such as Brooklyn, Harlem Heights and White Plains. Washington, however, always managed to avoid surrender and thus kept his ragged, ill-equipped army in being. This phase of the war was concluded by the ill-fated advance from Canada by General Burgoyne, which ended with his surrender at Saratoga on October 17, 1777.

The second half of the war was fought mainly in the south. Clinton took over from Howe in 1778, just about the time that France came into the war on the side of the colonists, and the following year he decided to pull back to New York, and then concentrate his efforts in the south. Early in 1780 he set sail for Charleston, which he captured after a short siege. The 33rd distinguished themselves at small loss to themselves, losing only one man killed and two wounded, but were specially marked out by the commander-in-chief for his congratulations. Clinton then returned to New York, handing over command of active operations to

Cornwallis. There followed nearly a year of hard marching and hard fighting for the 33rd. Cornwallis was a demanding commander, but he had the confidence of his troops. At Guildford Court House in North Carolina, on March 15, 1781, the 33rd were involved in one of the hardest battles in all their history, in the course of which they lost their commanding officer, Lieutenant-Colonel Webster, and nearly 100 killed or wounded. They fought alongside the Guards against one of the best of the American regiments, the 1st Maryland, and held their position throughout the day. But Cornwallis's losses had been heavy and there was little hope of reinforcement.

Cornwallis then decided to carry the war into Virginia, a decision for which he was criticized at the time by Clinton, because it meant uncovering his main base at Charleston, and for which he has been criticized since. At first all went well, but he was forced eventually to retire to Yorktown, not far from the state capital of Williamsburg, and wait for reinforcements. Any hope of reinforcement was, however, lost by the British temporary loss of command of the sea, and instead of the Royal Navy lying off Yorktown, Cornwallis found the French. This sealed the fate of the British and German garrison under Cornwallis, although the siege of Yorktown lasted from October 6 until October 17. Washington commanded the Americans at Yorktown, and Rochambeau the considerable French contingent; they out-numbered and out-gunned the British, who were losing men daily through sickness and enemy action.

The storming by the French and Americans of two key redoubts on the night of October 14, and the failure of an attempt to evacuate the garrison across the York River to Gloucester Point, decided Cornwallis that further resistance was useless. He asked Washington for terms on October 17, and on October 19 the garrison marched out to lay down their arms in what has since come to be known as 'Surrender Field'. They were not allowed to march out with colours flying, nor were their bands allowed to play either an American or French march. The British, and their German comrades, therefore, left Yorktown with their fifes and drums playing 'The World Turned Upside Down,' and led by General O'Hara, Cornwallis's second-in-command. Cornwallis himself managed to avoid the surrender ceremony by pleading illness, and was much criticized for this later.

Neither the 33rd, nor their comrades, were convinced that surrender was necessary. There were sad hearts when the command was given: 'Present arms! Lay down arms! Put off swords and cartridge-boxes!' A Corporal in the 76th (Macdonald's) Highlanders, which also formed part of the garrison, clasped his weapon to his breast before throwing it down, saying, 'May you never get so good a master!' The Regiment lost 28 killed, wounded and missing at Yorktown, and were then destined to spend many months as prisoners of war until peace was signed a year later in November, 1782. The surrender at Yorktown, which took place on the anniversary of Burgoyne's surrender at Saratoga, was in fact the climactic moment of the first British Empire, just as the fall of Singapore was of the second. Although George III received the news of Yorktown with firmness and fortitude, his Prime Minister, Lord North, greeted the news with, 'Oh God! it is all over!' It was one of the few occasions during his conduct of the American War when Lord North turned out to be correct.

★　　★　　★

The 33rd were only about 160 strong when they returned from America and were sent to Taunton. They had managed to retain their Colours and brought them home with them, much torn and tattered after hard service in America; they were eventually deposited in the Church of St Mary Magdalene in Taunton. New Colours were presented in Taunton in 1783. It was while they were in Taunton that the Regiment's connection with the West Riding of Yorkshire was officially confirmed. In 1782 infantry regiments were asked to state their preference if county titles were to be allocated, and in a letter dated July 1, 1782 Cornwallis replied:

> 'I am to desire that you will please to inform General Conway that the 33rd Regt of Infantry has always recruited in the West Riding of Yorkshire, and has a very good interest, and the general good will of the people, in that part of the Country: I should therefore wish not only to be permitted to recruit in that county, but that my regt. may bear the name of the 33rd or West Yorkshire Regt.; If that district is thought too extensive to give a name to one regt. only, I should desire to have my regt. called the 1st West Yorkshire; and am fully sure that no older regt. can claim so long and intimate connection with the West Riding of Yorkshire.'

An order was shortly issued conferring on the 33rd the title 'First Yorkshire West Riding Regiment', thereby formally establishing a connection which the intervening

The Havercake

years have strengthened and which is as valued as much by the Dukes as it is by the people of the West Riding.

It was at about this time that the 33rd acquired the nickname of 'Havercake Lads'. Although much better known today as the 'Dukes', there was a time when the nickname 'Havercake Lads' was quite widely used inside the army. The 'Havercake' is a large oatcake, once peculiar to the West Riding, and recruiting sergeants used to stick these on the points of their swords when combing the inns and alleys for recruits. Not that recruits were often forthcoming—they needed more than a 'Havercake' to tempt them to take the king's shilling, which is hardly surprising when one learns that the soldier's spending money was rather less than one pound a year. Even if one takes into account the vast difference in the purchasing power of the pound between those days and these, it can scarcely be claimed that the country paid its soldiers handsomely for the privilege of dying for it. Nor did it take much more care for their accommodation, any old barn being fit for the soldiery, while the barracks were, if anything, worse, men often sleeping four or five to a bunk. But for all these hardships, men still took infinite pride in their regiments, and in the eighty years of its existence the 33rd Foot had given those serving in its ranks much to be proud about.

Chapter
2

The 33rd Foot and the Duke of Wellington

THE 33rd were in Dublin in 1793, when the Honourable Arthur Wesley (later Wellesley), then a captain in the 18th Light Dragoons and serving as an ADC to the Lord Lieutenant of Ireland, purchased a majority into the Regiment with money he had borrowed from his brother Richard, Earl of Mornington. Arthur Wesley was aged 24 and had risen from Ensign to Major in six years without once hearing a shot fired in anger; nor, for that matter, had he received much instruction in the details of his chosen profession. As a result of the system then prevailing in the British Army of purchasing commissions, and subsequent steps in rank, young Wesley had moved in rapid succession through the 73rd Highlanders, 41st Foot, 76th Foot, 12th Light Dragoons, 58th Foot, and 18th Light Dragoons. He joined the 33rd Foot as a Major on April 30, 1793, and purchased the Lieutenant-Colonelcy five months later, again with money lent by the obliging Richard.

The Morningtons were not a rich family by the standards of the nobility in those days, and Arthur Wesley had risen slowly when compared with some of his richer contemporaries. He was also in debt, and was hard-pressed to settle outstanding regimental accounts with the 33rd's Military Agents. Cornwallis, Colonel of the 33rd and now Governor-General in Bengal, owed the Agents 'the enormous balance' of £3,039. 9s. 1¼d. which caused the Agents to complain querulously: 'we never had a Regiment that left this Establishment with their accounts in so unsettled a manner.'

1793 was a memorable year for both the 33rd and the future Duke of Wellington. The Regiment was beginning its association with one of this country's greatest soldiers from whom it was later to take its unique title; while Wesley, disappointed in love, for he had been refused the hand of Kitty Pakenham because her family believed he could not keep her on an army officer's pay,* was about to begin the military career which was to culminate in the acknowledgement that he was one of the two greatest soldiers in Europe. Napoleon was the other.

He learnt his trade in a hard school, and the 33rd with him. War had broken out between Britain and France after the execution of King Louis XVI, and an expeditionary force was sent to Holland under the Duke of York. It is a campaign best remembered for the incompetence of the generals and the miseries suffered by the troops. The 33rd sailed from Cork for Ostend in late May, 1794 to take part in these disastrous operations. They could hardly have arrived at a more inopportune moment, since the main body of the army was involved in a disorderly retreat across Belgium towards the Scheldt.† The rain poured down ceaselessly, the local inhabitants openly favoured the French, while the British regiments were a hotch-potch of veterans and raw recruits—'many of them do not know one end of a firelock from the other, and will never know it.' The supply system was virtually non-existent, no provision had been made for the issue of winter clothing, and the infamous traffic in officers' commissions by Army brokers during the previous ten years had resulted in as useless a collection of officers as the British Army has ever known.

The campaign is chiefly remembered for having inspired the satiric lines:

* They were eventually married on April 10, 1806. By then he was Major-General The Hon. Sir Arthur Wellesley, K.B. It did not turn out to be the happiest of matches.

† Similarly confused conditions greeted the 2nd Battalion of the Dukes when they landed in Burma in February, 1942.

The Noble Duke of York,
He had ten thousand men,
He marched them up to the top of the hill,
And he marched them down again.

But it should also be memorable for the engagement at Boxtel, in Holland, on September 15, 1794, because this was the first time Arthur Wesley came under enemy fire. He acquitted himself well. The French cavalry were advancing to charge at a moment when the retreating British cavalry had become inextricably mixed with a battalion of the Guards. There was great confusion, but Lieutenant-Colonel Wesley kept his head. He deployed the 33rd in line, allowed the retreating cavalry and Guards to pass through, then re-formed into line and drove back the French with a series of well-controlled volleys.

Shortly after the engagement at Boxtel the Duke of York took himself off to London to argue the requirements of his army with a government more bent on economy than victory. He left his troops to endure the coldest winter in living memory, which they might confidently have expected to spend in the comparative warmth of winter quarters. However, the ragged soldiers of the French Revolution were not fettered by past conventions. They broke all the rules by advancing along the frozen canals, hunting the British, Dutch and German soldiers out of their warm billets, and driving them helter-skelter through Holland and across the northern German plains in sub-arctic temperatures. The retreat began on January 17 and did not end until the British reached Bremen in March.

Lieutenant-Colonel Wesley was one of the few to emerge from the campaign with his military reputation unimpaired, but it left him with the poorest opinion of his generals. Although the 33rd were at one stage billeted within 30 miles of headquarters, they were never once visited by the Commander-in-Chief, whose staff whiled away the long winter nights with a good deal of wine, women and song.

'The infantry regiments' Wesley recalled many years later, 'were as good in proper hands as they are now [1837], but the system was wretched.' Later still, when asked if he had found the campaign useful, he replied: 'Why—I learnt what one ought not to do, and that is always something.'

The 33rd were back in England in May, 1795 decimated by cold, disease and starvation. Wesley's first task was to recruit them up to strength, although he too was suffering from the effects of the campaign. He was undecided whether to abandon the army for politics, but the 33rd were under orders for the West Indies and he decided to accompany them there. The expedition, however, did not get far, seven transports being wrecked on Chesil Beach while the rest were storm-bound in Portsmouth Roads. The orders were then changed for India, and the 33rd sailed in April, 1796 leaving behind their colonel (Wesley had already purchased the next step in rank), as he was still sick. He hurried after them, catching up at Cape Town, and taking with him a chestful of books for reading on the voyage. They had cost him £50 and doubtless contributed to the £955. 14s. 8d. he owed to the Mornington family agent: he was also heavily in debt to his brother, Richard.

India was not reached until February, 1797 after a voyage described by Wesley as 'most tedious'. The 33rd were stationed in Fort William, Calcutta, where the social season was at its height, prior to the onset of the hot weather, and the officers of the 33rd and their colonel were soon to show that no ball or banquet was complete without them. It is difficult to understand how anyone survived the wining and dining of those days in India. Men dressed in much the same fashion as in Europe—tight-fitting coats, knee-breeches and wigs. There was no air-conditioning and ice was a luxury. Dinners began at 4 p.m. and went on until the small hours, with roast beef, plum puddings and all the trimmings. Toasts were drunk 'three times' three' and it was not considered a party unless every guest was carried home drunk. William Hickey has described a party he attended with the 33rd, at which he found himself drinking with 'eight as strong-headed fellows as could be found in Hindustan'; he staggered home at 2 a.m. with an excruciating hang-over which lasted forty-eight hours. 'Indeed, a more severe debauch I never was engaged in in any part of the world,' he recorded with evident satisfaction, and presumably Colonel Wesley and his officers felt the same. Unfortunately we have no record of how the rank and file of the 33rd passed their time, but probably in much the same fashion as their officers, only in their case country liquor took the place of champagne and claret and killed the more quickly.

Even today, with every modern invention to alleviate it, Calcutta's climate remains unpleasant. It was infinitely more so for Europeans in 1797 when the 33rd Foot sweated it out in gloomy and insanitary barrackrooms inside Fort William. There was hardly any field training, as we understand the term, but hours were spent on the drill square; and there were guards to be mounted on the Governor-General's palace and on other public buildings. The officers, with so much time to kill, gambled recklessly, and the colonel of the 33rd had to rescue more than one of his junior officers from the results of folly with the cards. And there were, of course, the numerous funerals; the British government did not pay well, but they interred their deceased officers and soldiers with pomp and ceremonial. Between January 1, 1793 and December 31, 1798 the 33rd lost 430 men dead, only six of whom had been killed in action, and there was therefore plenty of practice for the bearer parties.

The boredom of garrison life was such that everyone longed for action. At first it seemed that this would come in the Phillipines. An expedition was being prepared to capture Manila and Colonel Wesley had hopes of commanding it; but the expedition was recalled before it had passed through the Malacca Straits. This was because the home government was alarmed by the prospect of increased French intervention in India. Colonel Wesley and the 33rd returned to Fort William, but he had at least the satisfaction of knowing that his eldest brother was shortly to arrive in Calcutta as Governor-General. Lord Mornington had already decided to change the family name from Wesley to Wellesley, and the first time Colonel Arthur Wellesley signed his name as such was on May 19, 1798 in a letter to General Harris in Madras informing him of the safe arrival of the Earl of Mornington in Calcutta.

The wars between the British and French in India were basically of commercial origin, each nation espousing the cause of some Indian potentate in the hope that it would benefit commercially. For such fighting as might result both the British and French depended mainly on Indian, or Sepoy, regiments, trained on the European model and officered by Europeans; these Sepoy armies were stiffened by small bodies of European troops. The numerous Indian princes maintained their own armies, ill-disciplined and usually ill-trained, but in almost every case there would be a *corps d'élite* of picked troops, trained by European advisers and commanded by them in battle. By the end of the eighteenth century the British were gradually ousting the French and to that extent were the more to be feared by the Indians; for this reason French influence was in the ascendant at those Indian courts which feared annexation by the East India Company, and prominent among these princes was Tipu Sultan, ruler of the great state of Mysore in southern India.

Tipu, a Moslem ruling a predominantly Hindu state, had clashed before with the British. Cornwallis captured his capital at Seringapatam in 1793 and Tipu had been fortunate to escape with only some minor loss in territory; Cornwallis, at that time Governor-General, was opposed to further increase in the Company's territory, but the same was certainly not true of the Earl of Mornington. When he decided in February, 1799 to regard Tipu Sultan's negotiations with Napoleon as an excuse for war, he had no illusions about the object of the campaign, which was the overthrow of Tipu's dynasty and the substitution of British influence for any other in Mysore. He took the precaution of sending his brother Arthur, together with the 33rd, to Madras, where they arrived in August, 1798 after a hair-raising voyage. Their transport ran on to a reef and they narrowly escaped drowning: as if this was not enough, bad water on the ship gave them all 'the flux'—from which '15 as fine men as any we had' died. The formidable Colonel Wellesley was very angry.

Fort St George in Madras was to be the 33rd's base for the next eleven years, although the Regiment spent comparatively little time in the fort itself. Probably nowhere else in India is there a place more redolent of the British connection than Fort St George, with its 300 year-old church (the oldest Anglican church in India) containing Clive's marriage lines in its parish registry, as well as Colonel Arthur Wellesley's signature as witness to a marriage. There is also the house where Wellesley lived while preparing the force for the campaign against Tipu, a task he performed so well that when General Harris arrived in February, 1799, to take over command, he found 'one of the best organized and disciplined armies ready to receive him that had ever taken the field in India'. The Governor-General would probably have been happier if Colonel Wellesley could have been appointed commander-in-chief, but not even in those days of jobbery and nepotism could this have been contrived. Colonel Wellesley was only just 30, and had the ill-starred campaign in Holland as his only claim to operational experience; Harris, on the other hand, was a veteran who had commanded the 76th Foot at Seringapatam in 1793. Wellesley resented the cavalier fashion with which Harris treated him, after all his hard work in organizing the troops, but he certainly did not allow this to affect his reaction to the Earl of Mornington's proposal to take the field in person. 'All I can say upon the subject is,' he wrote to Calcutta, 'that if I were in General Harris's situation, and you joined the army, I should quit it.' The Governor-General did not pursue the subject.

Virtue was to have its reward. The Nizam of Hyderabad, greatest of the Indian princes, had been intriguing with the French. A mixture of diplomacy and threats, coupled with some insolent behaviour by Tipu, brought him over to the British. He had a large, European-trained army which would be useful in the campaign against Tipu, but he stipulated that it should be commanded by a British officer. Colonel Wellesley was given the command, and set off for Hyderabad from Madras taking the 33rd with him, under the command of Major Shee.

Wellesley and Shee were not the happiest of combinations. Shee possessed an Irish temper that rapidly reached boiling point; Wellesley on the other hand, even thus early in his career, always had his emotions well in hand, but his sarcasm had a cutting edge. He found fault with some men of the 33rd for marching without arms and equipment (a not uncommon fault in India where soldiers could always find some follower to carry their arms for them) and remonstrated with Major Shee. Shee objected to the censure and received a sharp reply: 'This is not the first time I have had occasion to observe that, under forms of private correspondence, you have written me letters upon public duty, couched in terms to which I have not been accustomed.' He threatened to send any similar letters to the commander-in-chief and Shee flew into a rage and demanded a court-martial. It was hardly an auspicious beginning to an arduous campaign.

The Hyderabad contingent, as might have been expected, was not organized in accordance with the standards demanded by Colonel Wellesley. Its vast impedimenta was carted by bullocks which died in droves, and it crawled across the Indian countryside like an undisciplined horde. There was, too, a great deal of confusion in coordinating the tri-pronged advance on Seringapatam—General Harris coming from the east, Wellesley from the north, and General Stuart with a Bombay contingent from the west. Eventually, however, the slow-moving columns were assembled around Seringapatam, but not before steady volleys from the 33rd had repulsed a determined attack by Tipu's picked troops at Mallavelly on March 26. It was to prove a foretaste of what was to be expected in the storming of Seringapatam, for Tipu's soldiers had fought like tigers.

On the night of April 5, Wellesley was ordered to clear an enemy outpost located in a thick orchard outside the fortress walls. There was no time for reconnaissance, Wellesley became separated in the dark from the 33rd and was temporarily lost, while the 33rd ran into murderous enemy fire and were forced to retire. Eight of their men were captured, taken into the fortress, and executed by strangling or by having nails driven into the tops of their skulls. This unfortunate action made such an impression on Wellesley that he later wrote to the Governor-General: 'I have come to a determination; when in my power, never to suffer an attack to be made by night upon an enemy who is . . . strongly posted, and whose posts have not been reconnoitred by daylight.'

The situation was retrieved the following morning by a daylight attack on the orchard, and the British then settled down to reduce Seringapatam by siege warfare. The assault took place early in the morning of May 4, 1799, led by General Baird, who had old scores to settle; he had spent nearly three years in Seringapatam as Tipu's prisoner. The 33rd stormed through the breaches into one of the strongest fortresses in India and hunted the defenders through a labyrinth of buildings, pleasure gardens, and bazaars. Tipu's body was not found until later, tracked down by Baird, who was accompanied by Wellesley, while Tipu's wives and children were escorted to safety by the Light Company of the 33rd. Next morning, to the fury of General Baird, Colonel Arthur Wellesley was appointed Governor of Seringapatam, and at once set about restoring order among the troops, who were fast running amok. His share of the prize money was £4,000 (General Harris received £150,000), while a private in the 33rd received £18, plus, of course, whatever he managed to conceal before the prize-agents and the provost-marshal had time to frisk him.

Colonel Arthur Wellesley now had his foot firmly set on the ladder which was to bring him distinction in the first Mahratta War, which began in 1803. He was employed during the three intervening years in a series of minor campaigns in southern India, in few of which he was accompanied by the 33rd, who were condemned to a round of humdrum garrison duties. During this period the conduct of Colonel Shee became increasingly erratic, and his officers seem to have taken their cue from him. There was a furious row one Christmas because a major's servant had over-charged the lieutenant-colonel's for fifty raisins in his plum pudding, and an unfortunate instance of an officer 'staggering on parade' due to a sudden 'indisposition'. The 33rd were certainly maintaining their reputation for hard drinking, and at a dinner given in honour of Wellesley's promotion to Major-General (he was promoted on the Indian establishment on April 29, 1802), one of the subalterns in his cups said something so awful that he was 'sent to Coventry' by the rest of the mess. Wellesley blamed most of this misbehaviour on Shee, whose example was there for all to see, and was as relieved as the rest of the regiment when that liverish officer died from a 'spasmodic fit' which took several days to kill him. It was not a very happy chapter in the history of the 33rd.

When Lord Cornwallis died in June, 1806, Sir Arthur Wellesley, who had served as Lieutenant-Colonel in the 33rd for thirteen years, succeeded Cornwallis as Colonel of the Regiment. He returned to England in 1805, but seven more years were to pass before the 33rd sailed for home at the end of their Indian service. They had won the battle honour of 'Seringapatam' but had seen little action during the latter part of their service in India. They were particularly disappointed not to have served under Wellesley during his victorious campaign against the Mahrattas, but he continued to take as keen an interest in the Regiment as when they were serving under his direct command.

★   ★   ★

After their return from India the 33rd had barely a year a home before setting off again on their travels—this time to the Continent, where Napoleon's empire was falling apart after his defeat at Leipzig in October, 1813. They were involved in an abortive attack on Bergen-op-Zoom, one of the strongest fortresses in Holland, and shortly afterwards Napoleon was exiled to Elba. The 33rd then went into garrison in Flanders. Their former Colonel, now the Duke of Wellington, had given up the Colonelcy in February, 1813 when he was appointed Colonel of the Royal Horse Guards (The Blues), and was succeeded by Lieutenant-General Sir John Sherbrooke, 'a short, square, hardy little man,' who had once been a captain in the 33rd. Wellington considered him to be 'a very good officer, but the most passionate man [he] ever knew.' Sherbrooke had been 2nd lieutenant-colonel in the 33rd in 1796 when Wellington was 1st lieutenant-colonel.

The diplomats in Vienna, who were trying to put together the shattered pieces of Europe, were shaken out of their deliberations on March 11, 1815, when they heard of Napoleon's escape from Elba and return to France. Once more the armies were put in motion and Wellington abandoned diplomacy to take command of the British-Dutch-Belgian forces assembling in Belgium. The 33rd were at Oudenarde at this time and were placed in the 5th

Brigade under Major-General Sir Colin Halkett.* The commanding officer was Lieutenant-Colonel Elphinstone.†

Napoleon, having re-raised his army in a remarkably short time, concentrated it at Charleroi on the Franco-Belgian frontier. His aim was to defeat Wellington and the Prussians under Blücher, before turning his attention to the Austrians and Russians who were also concentrating against him. Wellington, uncertain whether Napoleon would move first against Blücher or himself, and equally uncertain which route Napoleon would take, kept his options open until the last possible moment. He had, however, already decided that if Napoleon advanced on Brussels by the most direct route from Charleroi he would fight him along the ridge of Mont St Jean, not far from the village of Waterloo, on the southern edge of the Forest of Soignes.

In the event Napoleon took Wellington by surprise by advancing more rapidly than Wellington expected, and by making his main effort against the Prussians, whom he severely mauled at Ligny on June 16. Wellington reacted quickly but it was as much by luck as by good management that sufficient troops were concentrated at Quatre Bras, a vital crossroads 12 miles south of Waterloo, in time to prevent Marshal Ney pushing up the Charleroi-Brussels highway. Quatre Bras was a most confusing battle, regiments being thrown into the conflict as they came up from the line of march, and it was not until the late afternoon of June 16 that the 33rd, who had marched out of Soignies the previous day, deployed on to the battlefield. They arrived at an unfortunate moment as the 69th Foot, who had been deployed in line instead of in square by the Prince of Orange to deal with a French cavalry charge, broke and fell back in disorder

* 5th Brigade consisted of the 33rd, and the second battalions of the 30th, 69th, and 73rd Foot.
† Elphinstone later commanded the 16th (The Queen's) Light Dragoons, but is better remembered for his incompetence when commanding the force in Kabul which was massacred by the Afghans in January, 1842. He died a prisoner in Afghan hands.

carrying the 33rd with them into Bossu Wood, where the cavalry could not follow them. They re-formed under the protections of the trees, and later moved forward in support of a charge by the Guards which restored the situation on that part of the front. During this unfortunate affair the 33rd suffered over 100 casualties, including ten officers killed or wounded.

Fortunately, Ney displayed very little tactical skill at Quatre Bras, while Napoleon was so heavily engaged with the Prussians that he paid little attention to the actions of his subordinates. The battle ended with Wellington still in possession of the cross-roads, and he was able to withdraw his troops the following day in good order. The French pursuit was hampered by a violent thunder-storm which turned the fields into quagmires through which the 33rd squelched, slipped and slithered as they made their way back to their next position—on the reverse slope of the Mont St Jean Ridge, to the right of centre of Wellington's line, and a few hundred yards north of the château of Hougoumont on the Nivelles-Brussels road.

A casual visitor to Waterloo today might be forgiven if he came away with the impression that the main contestants were the Belgians (under the Prince of Orange) and the French (under Napoleon). There is so little evidence of British (and Prussian) participation that it is difficult to appreciate that Waterloo was the greatest victory won by the British on land between Blenheim and El Alamein. It ended for ever Napoleon's hopes of establishing a French hegemony over Europe and securely established Wellington as one of the greatest captains in British military history. It is therefore particularly appropriate that the 33rd, Wellington's own regiment, should have been present on the occasion of his greatest triumph, and that they should have taken part in the final infantry charge that broke the ranks of the Imperial Guard and made victory certain. They lost 7 officers killed and 15 wounded, out of a total of 36 present

The Waterloo Medal

at Waterloo, and more than half the rank and file were either killed or wounded. For much of the day they remained just behind the crest of the ridge, either lying down to avoid the cannon and musket fire passing overhead, or formed in square to repel the French cavalry milling around them. The 5th Brigade held a vital sector of Wellington's line but there was little glory to be won standing there and watching the cannon balls as they ploughed a gory path through the ranks; and yet, as men fell to right and left, the remainder closed up on the centre to present an unbroken phalanx of bayonets.

At an early stage in the battle the Duke of Wellington reined in his horse beside the 33rd, who were then drawn up in square formation, and an old soldier, who had served with him in India, shouted, 'Let us have a huzza for our old Colonel!' The soldiers cheered heartily but the Duke (who loathed 'that damned cheering') held up his hand and said, 'Hush! Hush!' The cheering stopped instantly. Much later in the battle Wellington once again drew up beside the 33rd. He enquired from Halkett how the troops in his brigade were faring. 'My Lord,' said Halkett, 'we are dreadfully cut up. Can you not relieve us for a little while?' 'Impossible,' said the Duke curtly, 'Very well, my Lord,' said Halkett, "we'll stand till the last man falls,' and the Duke galloped off. Meanwhile the artillery fire, now at almost point-blank range, tore ever increasing gaps in the tight little squares of infantry, the cries of the wounded and dying rising even above the thunder of the guns.

It was between 6 and 7 p.m. that Napoleon launched the Imperial Guard, convinced that this would clinch the victory. As the tall, bear-skinned warriors tramped steadily up the ridge past the debris of battle, led by a hat-less Marshal Ney on foot, they were greeted by volley after controlled volley of musketry. Halkett's brigade was the dam against which their flood broke, and as the veterans of Marengo, Austerlitz and Jena hesitated, they were taken in the flank by Maitland's Guards and by Colborne's 52nd Foot. They wavered, and at that moment Halkett spurred forward to lead his brigade in the charge. He fell, wounded in the face, and Elphinstone took over command of the brigade. It was therefore left to a comparatively junior officer, Captain Knight, to command the 33rd at the decisive moment in the battle, and to bring them out of battle later.

Waterloo will always be one of the proudest battle honours

of the British Army, and the Dukes are rightly proud of their right to emblazon it on their Colours—and the more so because of their connection with the great soldier whose victory it was. The anniversary of the battle has always been celebrated in the regiment ever since.*

* There is a story, probably apocryphal, that on one such anniversary the regimental flag was flying from the turret over the Depot barracks at Halifax. The commanding officer of the Depot was inspecting a squad of new recruits and he picked on a raw young Yorkshireman to ask him why the flag was flying. After a long pause the recruit replied, ''Cos it's Waterloo Day.' The officer, delighted to have picked on such an intelligent recruit, went on to ask what had happened at Waterloo. There was an even longer pause, and much shuffling of feet, before the recruit replied. 'Ah doan't reetly knoaw but it's summat to do wi' whippets.'

It should be added for those who are unacquainted with north country sporting activities that the coursing of hares by whippets is very popular among the mining communities, and the premier greyhound coursing event in Britain is, of course, the Waterloo Cup.

Chapter
3
'Hindoostan'

T HE CHEQUERED career of the 76th Regiment of Foot
during the 125 years of the regiment's independent
existence provides as good an example as any of the
vagaries of British defence policy, and of the almost
ludicrous haste with which British government have reduced
the strength of the army as soon as it considered the immediate danger was past. The 76th Foot had, by 1881, been
raised three times, disbanded twice, and amalgamated once.
The regiment was to be amalgamated yet again, but by then
it had become the 2nd Battalion of the Duke of Wellington's
Regiment. The 76th were first raised in 1756 by George,
Lord Forbes as the 61st Foot and renumbered 76th in 1758.
They took part in the siege of Belle Isle in 1761, and the
capture of Martinique in 1762, before being disbanded in
1763. Four years later the regiment reappeared in the Army
List as the 76th Macdonald's Highlanders. It fought well in
the American War of Independence, often alongside the
33rd, and was involved in the surrender at Yorktown; it was
disbanded at Stirling Castle in 1784. The only link with the
76th Foot that came after is the pleasant legend that for
some time a piper was included in the establishment to
commemorate the Scottish connection, but there is nothing
to substantiate this.

There was then a gap of only three years before the third
incarnation of the 76th Foot. The Regiment was raised
specifically for service in India, largely because of the alarm
felt in London over French intrigues with Hyder Ali, the
Moslem adventurer who had made himself master of the

great state of Mysore in southern India. The East India Company disliked spending money on soldiers, and they particularly disliked having to pay for the King's regiments, as British Army units serving in India were called; they preferred to raise their own Sepoy regiments, which were much cheaper to maintain, backed up by a handful of wholly European regiments in the Company's pay. The Company therefore refused to pay for the 76th, and the three other British regiments raised for the same purpose, and they even went so far as to refuse them transportation in the Company's ships. William Pitt, who was then Prime Minister, was not the man to stand this kind of treatment from a body of merchants; he soon forced a bill through parliament compelling the Company not only to provide transportation, but also to defray the cost of raising and equipping the four regiments and of maintaining them all the time they were in India. The 76th were therefore raised on October 12, 1787, by Colonel Thomas Musgrave, and embarked at Gravesend on March 26 of the following year for India. Among the lieutenants shown on the muster roll was the 'Hon. Arthur Weslie' [sic], but he did not sail with the Regiment; he chose instead to return to his native Ireland as ADC to the Lord lieutenant, and shortly afterwards transferred to another regiment. However, it is of interest that the Duke of Wellington had this slight connection with the 76th, although, of course, his connection with the 33rd was of much longer duration.

Most regiments in the British Army have fought in India at one time or other, but no regiment won such distinction in so short a space of time as the 76th Foot, and no other is entitled to the battle honour 'Delhi 1803' to commemorate the capture by the British of the ancient capital of Hindustan. For the 76th Foot played an outstanding part in the campaigns which were to decide the mastery of India for the next 150 years—the war in Mysore against Tipu Sultan, son of Hyder Ali, and the first war against the Mahrattas.

Unfortunately these campaigns in India are not easy for the general reader to follow; the names of the battles are usually unpronounceable, while the distances involved in the marching and counter-marching can seldom be comprehended from the usual small scale-map. However an attempt must be made to describe the 76th's part, even if only in outline, since the full magnitude of the British effort in India in those early days of our rule is very imperfectly understood in Britain today.

India towards the end of the eighteenth century was in a state of chaos. This was largely due to the break-up of the Moghul Empire, which began to disintegrate after the death of Aurangzeb in 1707. The British settlements at Madras, Calcutta and Bombay were separated from each other by thousands of miles of roadless jungles, mountains and deserts. The only means of communication was by river or along execrable tracks. The pace was that of the bullock cart—two miles an hour in fair weather, and considerably less during the rains. Disease of every kind was endemic; dysentery and malaria killed far more swiftly and surely than bullets.

The British soldier could expect to remain in India for as much as 15 years or more without home leave. He probably employed a servant to look after his kit, and an Indian woman to cater for his other needs, but little concession was made for the climate. He wore much the same thick uniform as at home, was gaitered and trussed as securely as if on guard duty outside St James's, and very little attention was paid to his welfare. He spent much of his time drinking native spirits which rotted his guts, and he was lucky if he managed to survive the numerous diseases for more than a few years. Those who did survive the many health hazards usually lived to a great age, often settling in India, but a great many more died. When it came to campaigning they were expected to march great distances under a broiling sun, or plod through thick mud during the rainy season, and then storm the fortress of some recalcitrant rajah, knowing full well that under such climatic conditions the slightest scratch would become septic. The wonder is that any of them did survive, and even more surprising that so many British soldiers elected to remain in India with either another regiment, or in the Company's service, when the time came for their regiment to go home. The truth of the matter is, of course, that however hard the life may have been, the British soldier was a good deal better off in India than he ever was in his own country.

The 76th landed at Madras in July, 1788 after a remarkably quick voyage (less than four months) round the Cape of Good Hope. It must have been a merciful deliverance after the stinking transports, in which the soldiers were herded together like cattle and compelled to endure indescribable conditions whenever there were rough seas. The troop decks were kept clean by being washed with vinegar, and occasionally fumigated by smoking rags, while the soldiers were occupied by picking oakum on the deck and putting down an occasional mutiny by the crew. The officers were probably equally bored, but they did have the chance of an odd shot at an albatross, or a day's fishing in one of the ship's boats whenever the ship was becalmed.

The Regiment had hardly been in India six months before war broke out with Tipu Sultan, the ruler of Mysore. Tipu, aided and abetted by the French, was making a nuisance of himself by raiding the Company's territory and burning villages. An army of 15,000 men was concentrated at Madras in 1790, and later took part in some inconclusive manoeuvring against Tipu; neither side did much harm to each other, but the 76th, now 786 strong, marched many miles and became acclimatized to the sticky tropical heat of southern India. The following year the tempo quickened as a result of the arrival of the Governor-General, Lord Cornwallis, to take personal charge of the operations. He was not the kind of man to sit about waiting to be attacked, and soon the entire army was marching westwards against Bangalore, one of Tipu's main strongholds. The 76th had their baptism of fire at the storming of Bangalore—under Cornwallis, who was then Colonel of the 33rd—and they then moved on to attack Tipu's capital at Seringapatam.

The attack had to be abandoned on account of the incessant bad weather which killed off the baggage bullocks and disrupted the supply system; moreover the co-operation expected with a Mahratta army failed to materialize. Cornwallis decided to withdraw to Bangalore until he could build up supplies, and in the meantime employed his troops in reducing the numerous hill forts which menaced his communications and provided bolt-holes for Tipu's troops. The 76th distinguished themselves at the storming of Savandroog, north-west of Bangalore, which was known locally as the 'Hill of Death', not only on account of its supposedly impregnable position, but also because of the pestilential climate of the surrounding jungles. Despite its formidable reputation, Savandroog was stormed with the loss of only one man wounded, the garrison abandoning the fort as the storming parties from the 76th and 52nd Foot scrambled up the precipitous hillside. The stormers were encouraged by the 52nd's band playing 'Britons strike home', and both regiments were complimented by Cornwallis, although in his view 'the resistance was so contemptible'. Contemptible it may have been, but it taught the 76th a useful lesson early in their Indian service, which was that boldness usually paid in operations against the badly disciplined Indian levies.

Seringapatam was captured on February 23, 1792, after 15 days' siege. The 76th lost one officer killed and 12 officers and soldiers wounded. Soon afterwards they were ordered to march to Calcutta, over 1,000 miles away, while their commanding officer, Lieutenant-Colonel Harris, wisely took himself off to England for two years' leave. He later became Commander-in-Chief in Madras, and later still was given a peerage. Colonel Hon. W. Monson of the 52nd succeeded him in command of the 76th.

The East India Company was becoming deeply involved in the affairs of the province of Oudh, the heart-land of Hindustan from where it recruited many of its sepoys. Oudh enjoyed an unenviable reputation for misgovernment, and the peasantry were often on the verge of revolt against their rapacious landlords. In 1800 the 76th were moved to Cawnpore, on what was then the north-western frontier of the Company's territory, in order to be on hand if Oudh should burst into flames. It was to be their base for the next five years and they were joined there by Colonel Monson. Not long afterwards Lieutenant-General Lake (afterwards Lord Lake) arrived in Calcutta as Commander-in-Chief; his name will always be associated with the 76th Foot, for they were to win many hard-fought victories under his command.

The anarchic conditions in India led every petty rajah to try and extend his boundaries and consequently there were a series of minor campaigns in 1801 and 1802. These have become known as the 'Mud War', since they involved breaching and storming the mud-walled fortresses of the local chiefs. The garrisons seldom stood and fought it out but even so the breaching was often a hazardous operation. The 76th were involved in these operations and received favourable mention from General Lake, as well as extra pay for their conduct under extremely wet and cold conditions. They suffered more from disease than battle casualties, but these operations provided an excellent pipe-opener for the much more serious campaign the following year.

This was the first war with Mahrattas. This powerful Hindu confederacy controlled the Deccan and most of Central India and aimed to substitute their rule for that of the Moghuls over India. They watered their horses in the Jumna as it flowed past the walls of Delhi and Agra, and held the Moghul emperor, Shah Alam, as a virtual prisoner in his palace in Delhi. Their armies were trained, and sometimes commanded, by foreign mercenaries, mostly French, and a Frenchman, M. Perron, was the governor of the great tract of country lying between the rivers Ganges and Jumna. The Company's Governor-General, the Earl of Mornington, elder brother of the future Duke of Wellington, was determined to smash the Mahrattas and annex large portions of their territory. Operations began in the summer of 1803; Lord Lake commanded the main army in the north, while Sir Arthur Wellesley commanded in the south, where he was soon to display his outstanding military abilities, and indirectly to earn for himself the disparaging comment made many years later by Napoleon, that he was 'only a sepoy general'.

It was stiflingly hot when the 76th marched out of Cawnpore in August, 1803. The temperature was at least 110°F in the shade and the countryside was thick with dust rising in clouds above the marching troops, clogging their throats and causing an intolerable thirst. The monotonous call of the Brain-Fever Bird rose above the squeal of the fifes, while kites and vultures wheeled high above the column, waiting for the inevitable moment when a pack animal, or even a human, would collapse gasping, to die from the terrible heat. The thick scarlet coats turned black with sweat, the sun beat down on unprotected necks, and the firelock weighed heavier and heavier as the day's march progressed. The army was accompanied by thousands of Indian followers to cater for their every need—men, women and children—and there were almost as many pack animals, mostly bullocks, but elephants also, as well as camels, horses and donkeys. Meat was taken on the hoof, which meant great herds of sheep, goats and cattle, and all had to be protected against the Mahratta horsemen on the look-out for stragglers. The army, therefore, advanced in a huge rectangle, infantry and cavalry forming the front, rear and flanks, the artillery marching closed up to the front, the guns dragged by teams of elephants or bullocks; only the horse artillery pieces, or 'galloper guns', were horse-drawn. Lake's army totalled 10,500 soldiers, but it was accompanied by upwards of 100,000 followers who devastated the countryside like locusts. They also died like flies, contaminating the wells, and spreading dysentery far and wide.

Ally Ghur (now Aligarh) was the first real action. The fort was a very strong one, and the headquarters of M. Perron. The storming party had to advance across a wide and deep ditch along a narrow causeway which was under incessant fire from the walls above. There was then a long and winding passage, blocked at intervals by heavy doors which had to be blown in by guns at point-blank range. The 76th, bravely supported by the 4th Bengal Native Infantry, rushed forward at 4.30 a.m. on September 4, 1803, and fought their way into the fortress, which was stoutly defended. Colonel Monson was wounded, supposedly by a pike fired from a gun, and the 76th lost five officers killed. Their total casualties were 24 killed and 66 wounded, which was heavy by Indian standards, but they captured 281 guns and most of M. Perron's valuables and military stores. They were singled out for special mention in Lord Wellesley's* congratulatory dispatch to General Lake. They also received a favourable comment from Sir Arthur Wellesley who, when he heard of the capture of Ally Ghur, wrote in his dispatch —'I think that General Lake's capture of Ally Ghur is one the most extraordinary feats I have ever heard of in this country'.

Lake now continued his advance on Delhi and on September 11 was almost within sight of the walls of the Red Fort. But the way was barred by a large Mahratta army drawn up in a position of great strength, the flanks protected by swarms of light horsemen. M. Perron had by then decided to change sides, doubtless to retrieve some of his

---

* The Earl of Mornington became the Marquess Wellesley in 1799.

possessions lost at Ally Ghur, and he received a warmer welcome from Lake than his treachery merited. It was extremely hot, the men had marched 18 miles, and water was scarce. They were too exhausted, and the enemy were posted too strongly, for Lake to take the position by assault. He therefore sent forward his cavalry as a screen to mask the movements of his infantry, but as soon as the cavalry came within musket shot of the enemy they began to withdraw slowly. The Mahrattas seized the bait, left their earthworks, and poured across the plain to complete the *coup de grâce*. Whereupon the British cavalry drew away to the flanks, revealing the infantry drawn up in line, and marching steadily forward with their firelocks still 'on the shoulder'. Despite a galling fire from cannon balls, grape and canister, the 76th and their Sepoy comrades continued to advance, led by Lake on his horse. When they were less than 100 paces from the enemy they halted for a moment, fired a volley, and then charged with the bayonet. The enemy broke, and were sabred and speared by the cavalry as they fled across country towards the Jumna, in which many of them were drowned.

Lake entered Delhi twenty-four hours later, and the 76th camped beneath the city walls. The emperor, Shah Alam, came to beg the general's protection, and the British were now masters of the ancient capital of Hindustan. 3,000 of the enemy had been killed, and 58 guns and much treasure were captured. The 76th buried 34 of their comrades, and just under 100 were wounded, many of whom died later; the Regiment had suffered a quarter of the total casualties incurred by Lake's army and had well earned the unique battle honour of 'Delhi 1803'. Later, as will subsequently be explained, they were honoured by the Governor-General by the award of two Honorary Colours in recognition of their gallantry at Ally Ghur and Delhi.

Lake did not linger long in Delhi. After appointing Colonel Ochterlony, the future conqueror of the Gurkhas, as Resident, he set off down the Jumna for Agra, taking ten days to cover a distance which today's tourists visiting the Taj Mahal cover in less than four hours. The formidable fortress at Agra capitulated after a week's siege, yielding up 176 guns and £240,000 worth of rupees. The 76th suffered no casualties at Agra and morale was high. They had been present at the capture of the twin capitals of the Moghuls, Delhi and Agra, and better still had been rejoined by their popular colonel, William Monson, who had recovered from his wound. He rejoined while the Regiment was on the march to Agra and they turned out and gave him three cheers—which he said did him more good than all the doctors in the universe.

Despite their reverses the Mahrattas were still full of fight. Some of their best-trained battalions in the pay of Scindiah or Gwalior had not been involved at either Agra or Delhi, and were concentrated south-west of Agra where they threatened the British communications, being well-placed to recapture Delhi. Lake decided to destroy this force and marched from Agra on October 27. He took with him three regiments of British light cavalry, the 76th, five regiments of native cavalry, seven regiments of native infantry, and the Company's artillery. He came up with the enemy near the village of Leswarree in the early morning of November 1, after a very exhausting march. His plan was to hold the enemy with his cavalry until the infantry could catch up, but in the interval the Mahrattas changed position, unbeknown to Lake owing to the clouds of dust raised by the cavalry. When eventually the infantry came up, having marched 25 miles in nine hours, the 76th at once advanced and received the full weight of the enemy's artillery fire. A less well-trained regiment would have hesitated but the 76th pressed on, well supported by the 29th Light Dragoons, who charged right home and threw the Mahrattas into confusion. Lake then put himself at the head of the 76th, and together with two native battalions, led a charge which drove the enemy from their guns. It was at this stage in the battle that Major-General Ware, hastening up with the reserves, had his head removed by a cannon ball.

The battle ended at 4 p.m. and was one of the fiercest ever fought in India. The Mahrattas had fought with great resolution and courage. There had been many feats of endurance on the British side. The cavalry had marched 42 miles in 24 hours and were continuously in action from the moment they came up with the enemy; their horses were without food and water for nearly 20 hours. The infantry marched 65 miles in 48 hours and went into action for four hours' hard fighting after less than an hour's rest. Lake described the 76th in his dispatch as "this handful of heroes" [*sic*], but he did not do too badly himself. He was under fire throughout the battle, his horse was shot under him, his son who was acting as his ADC was wounded while holding his horse's stirrup for his father to mount, and he was shot at point-blank range by an enemy matchlock which did no more than burn his coat. 'On this, as on every former occasion,' wrote Lake, 'His Excellency beheld with admiration the heroic behaviour of the 76th Regiment, whose gallantry must ever leave a lasting impression on his mind.' The Regiment has few battle honours harder earned than 'Leswarree'.

There was a lull in the fighting after Leswarree, though Lake's troops were continually harassed by parties of horsemen who intercepted supply convoys and cut down any stragglers. However, the Mahrattas showed no signs of taking the field for the time being, and Lake therefore decided to withdraw his troops to Cawnpore for the hot weather of 1804. The 76th arrived there after a trying march during which many men died of heat-stroke, and this despite the fact that most of the marching was done by night. The campaign had lasted eleven months, in the course of which the Regiment had marched many hundreds of miles, stormed one fort, fought two decisive battles, and lost over

16 per cent of its strength from battle casualties and sickness. They had certainly earned some respite from campaigning.

But this was not to be. Hardly had they arrived in Cawnpore than the Mahratta chieftain, Holkar, raided Delhi with a strong force. The garrison was besieged, while Colonel Monson, who had been commanding the force intended to watch the Mahratta movements, had to beat a disastrous retreat, losing all his guns and baggage before he reached safety at Agra. Lake then decided to concentrate his force at Agra, and the 76th left Cawnpore again on September 3, 1804. They marched first to Agra, and then up the left bank of the Jumna to relieve Delhi. A soldier of the 76th was taken prisoner during this march and was taken before Holkar, and had his head cut off. His captor was rewarded with ten rupees, while the head was stuck on a spear and the nautch girls danced round it—a particularly grisly may-pole. Delhi was relieved after a gallant defence, and Lake set off in pursuit of Holkar. The 76th formed part of a force, under Major-General Fraser, which was given the task of watching the Mahratta infantry and guns which were on the territory of the Rajah of Bhurtpore, about 50 miles east of Agra. Bhurtpore was not a Mahratta, but a Jat who had thrown in his lot with the Mahrattas after a good deal of sitting on the fence.

The road to Bhurtpore was protected by the fortress of Deig, and on November 12th Fraser's force came up with a strong Mahratta force covering the fortress. There were some 24 infantry battalions, a large body of cavalry, and 180 guns. Fraser had the 76th, flank companies of the 22nd and the 1st Bengal European Regiment, two regiments of Native Cavalry, eight battalions of Native Infantry, and very few guns. Despite this difference in strength Fraser did not hesitate to attack, and paraded his force before dawn on November 13, 1804. He advanced in two columns, wheeled into line, the 76th and two battalions of Native Infantry forming the first line, and charged with the bayonet.

The 76th broke through the first line of enemy guns, advanced two miles and came under fire from the fort. While they were in this exposed situation, the second line of the British having been left far behind, a party of 28 men of the 76th, under Captain Norford, charged the enemy cavalry and drove them from the field. Unfortunately Norford was killed while cheering on his men.

It was now necessary to reduce the fortress of Deig, which involved bringing up more artillery. The garrison, however, evacuated the place on November 24 and made off towards Bhurtpore. The easy capture of the fort was followed by an advance to Bhurtpore, where Lake arrived with additional reinforcements early in January, 1805. Bhurtpore was sometimes called the 'Bulwark of Hindustan' and was one of the strongest defended cities in India. Lake had 7,500 men, as against an enemy garrison of nearer 50,000, but his principal weakness lay in artillery. He lacked the heavy guns needed to batter a breach in the thick mud walls, which merely crumbled when struck by light cannon balls, and both he and his troops were probably suffering from over-confidence. In the four months his army remained outside Bhurtpore there were four successive attempts to storm the walls, all of which failed at heavy cost. Lieutenant Templeton of the 76th—'a little man, but possessed of the heart of a lion'—led the forlorn hope on the last two occasions, but was killed in the act of placing a small Union Jack on an enemy bastion. Lake then decided to abandon any further attempt at assault, but resolved to starve the place into surrender, and this at once brought the Rajah to seek terms. He signed a treaty with the Company and hostilities ceased on April 10, 1805.

The 76th had lost 17 officers and 289 other ranks killed and wounded in the struggle for Bhurtpore, and the Regiment was suffering greatly from sickness. More than a third of the Regiment were sick, and it was moved to Futtehpur Sikri, near Agra, to be under cover for the rainy season.

Whilst there, orders were received for a return to England, and the 76th reached Calcutta by river boat and route march at the end of December, 1805. More than half the Regiment volunteered to remain in India with other regiments, but among the officers who decided to return with it was Lieutenant John Shipp, who had been promoted into the 76th by Lord Lake. Shipp had enlisted into the 22nd Regiment, with which he had taken part in the siege of Deig and Bhurtpore, and he has left a most readable account of his adventures.* He was clearly a favourite of Lake's, who gave him a commission in the field for his bravery at Bhurtpore as Ensign in the 65th Foot, before promoting him into the 76th. Unfortunately he ran into debt in England, resigned his commission, and re-enlisted in the 24th Dragoons. If even half his account of his adventures is true, he must have been a most remarkable character.

When the 76th Foot sailed home on February 21, 1806 after almost exactly 18 years' service in India, the Regiment had won a reputation which has certainly never been excelled by any British regiment in India. Not even the 39th Foot,† which bore on its colours the words *Primus in Indis* as witness of the part it had played in winning the battle of Plassey could claim a prouder record; indeed it would be necessary to compare the 76th's record with those of the Company's European regiments to find anything comparable. Only two men, it is believed, who had sailed with it from Gravesend in 1787 returned with it in 1806, both having been promoted from the ranks.

This record was acknowledged more rapidly than usual, largely due to the efforts of Colonel Monson who had led the 76th with such distinction. It was represented to the King that the 76th had captured the twin capitals of Hindu-

---

* *The Path to Glory* by John Shipp: Edited by C. J. Stranks (Chatto and Windus, London, 1969).

† The Dorset Regiment, now amalgamated with the Devonshire Regiment to form the Devons & Dorsets, Prince of Wales's Division.

stan, Agra and Delhi, and in the process had rescued the Moghul emperor from his enemies. King George III was graciously pleased to authorize the 76th in 1806 to bear the word 'Hindoostan' on its Colours, 'as a distinguished testimony of its good conduct and exemplary valour during the period of its services in India,' and in 1807 a further order authorized an elephant to be embroidered on the Colours.

Nor was this all. The Honorary Stand of Colours given by the East India Company in 1803 to the 76th Foot, in commemoration of their gallantry at Ally Ghur and Delhi, were presented to the Regiment in Jersey, where the 76th were garrisoned, on January 27, 1808. They were presented by General Don, and blessed by the Dean of Jersey, who began his address with the words, 'O soldiers, what a noble task is yours!' and went on to say that he could not gaze upon the 'banners (awful in their decay). . . . without a degree of veneration which my feelings will not allow me to express.' However, he was not sufficiently overcome to prevent him discoursing at length in similar vein, doubtless causing some of the harder characters in the ranks to shift their feet and mutter quite unprintable descriptions of the reverend gentleman.

According to the *Historical Records of the 76th 'Hindoostan' Regiment*, 'the Colours were of the most splendid description.' The battle honours 'Hindoostan,' 'Delhi,' 'Agra,' 'Leswaree' and 'Ally Ghur' were embroidered on them, as was 'the Elephant, while a handsome gilt plate was fixed to each colour staff with the following engraved on it:

'76th Regiment'

'These Colours were presented to the Regiment by the Chairman and Court of Directors of the Honourable the East India Company, in testimony of its meritorious services and distinguished bravery in the different actions recorded upon them.'

At least the 76th could not complain that its gallant services had gone unremarked, as was usually the case in the

British Army in those days. The grant of a stand of Honorary Colours was indeed a unique distinction, and has been jealously regarded from that day to this. For the officers and soldiers who had marched so far, and who had fought so gallantly, they were a tangible acknowledgement of what they had achieved, but perhaps, if asked, they would have valued two things more. One was the nickname they had earned for themselves, 'The Immortals,' because it was said they had fought in so many battles and sieges that their enemy considered them to be proof against their bullets. The second was the saying, attributed to General Lake: 'Bring me my boots and the 76th Regiment of Foot and I am ready to do anything and go anywhere.'

Chapter

4

Named after a Subject

THE 76th Foot were not present at Waterloo, being involved at the time in Britain's meaningless war with the United States. They had spent little time at home after their return from India, embarking for Spain in September, 1808, and taking with them the Honorary Colours presented by the East India Company; they were not to receive regulation Colours until 1830. The object of the expedition to Spain was to support the Spaniards in their revolt against the French, and to combine with them in driving the French out of the Peninsula. Unfortunately it did not work out like that. Sir John Moore had to beat a hasty retreat across the mountains in appalling weather and re-embark his troops at Corunna, where he lost his life. The 76th emerged from this ordeal with their reputation unimpaired, but they lost their commanding officer, Colonel Symes, from exhaustion soon after their re-embarkation.

Hardly had the Regiment returned home than it was off again—this time to the island of Walcheren in Holland. A large force had been assembled under Lord Chatham, son of the great William Pitt but an unsuccessful general. His naval colleague was Admiral Strachan and between them they managed to bungle the enterprise beyond redemption. Their conduct of the campaign inspired the lampoon:

> 'Great Chatham with his sabre drawn
> Stood waiting for Sir Richard Strachan,
> Sir Richard longing to be at 'em,
> Stood waiting for the Earl of Chatham'

Sickness soon immobilized the troops, and by November, 1809, the 76th had 107 men in hospital, while 539 had been evacuated sick to England. Fortunately the expedition was abandoned before the 76th, already reduced to a skeleton, were completely wiped out.

The following three years were spent in Ireland, and they were at Kinsale when their first Colonel, Sir Thomas Musgrave, died on December 31, 1812, bequeathing £10 a year to the regimental school. The commanding officer issued a regimental order lamenting Sir Thomas's death and hoped that 'the Officers will concur with him in paying a slight mark of their regret, and respect for his memory, by wearing crape round their arm for one month, beginning on Saturday next.'

1813 was the year when Napoleon was fighting desperately to retain his throne and when Wellington was gaining the upper hand in Spain. The 76th joined the Peninsular army in August in time to take part in the siege of San Sebastian, and was one of the first British regiments to cross the Bidassoa and enter France. The Regiment was present at the Battle of Nivelle, although not heavily engaged, and played a prominent part at Nive, which was one of the few occasions in Spain when Wellington allowed his generals to conduct a battle on their own. By the time the war ended the 76th had added 'Peninsula' and 'Nive' to their battle honours.

There was much glory to be won in the Peninsula, even for regiments that came late to the campaign like the 76th, but there was little glory in the 76th's next campaign, best remembered for the burning of the Capitol in Washington by the British. 'The War of 1812', as it is sometimes known, was a futile contest; little military ability was displayed on either side and the splendidly-trained Peninsular veterans were frittered away. At Plattsburg on September 11, 1814 the 76th behaved with great gallantry, on the anniversary of their capture of Delhi, and were highly indignant when ordered to withdraw. The withdrawal of the British force was not a very creditable affair, over 500 men leaving the ranks, but the 76th were proud that not a man from the Regiment deserted. The war ended soon afterwards, and

An officer of the 33rd (1st Yorkshire West Riding) 1853

with it active service for the 76th after 27 years of almost continuous campaigning.

The successful conclusion of the long war against France resulted in an equally long period of peace, during which both the 33rd and the 76th were employed mainly in garrison duties at home and overseas. It was a time of military stagnation; generals served on into their seventies, economies reduced regiments to skeletons, and more attention was paid to the minutiae of dress regulations than to the improvement of the scandalous conditions of service. The life of soldiers in their barracks was compared disadvantageously with that of slaves on a West Indian plantation, and recruits were so slow in coming forward that men perforce served on until they were long past their duties. It was during this period that the Duke of Cambridge, cousin of Queen Victoria, spent some time at regimental duty with the 33rd in Gibraltar.

The Duke of Wellington died on September 14, 1852, after a life-time of service to his country. Probably only one other Englishman in modern times has made as much impact on the imagination of his fellow-countrymen—Sir Winston Churchill; Wellington's funeral, like Churchill's, was an occasion for national mourning, and the 33rd were brought from Manchester to take part in it. Shortly thereafter there was issued a General Order, on the anniversary of Wellington's greatest victory, which read as follows:

Horse Guards
18th June, 1853

Her Majesty has been graciously pleased to command that the 33rd Regiment of Foot shall henceforward bear the name of THE 33RD (or THE DUKE OF WELLINGTON'S) REGIMENT, which honourable distinction will be inscribed on the Colours of the Regiment.

By Command of the Right Honourable General Viscount Hardinge, Commanding in Chief.

G. BROWN
(Adjutant General)

The next campaign in which the 33rd were involved was the Crimean War—generally regarded as being one of the most misguided operations in British history. Additional support has been lent to this view by that excellent book, *The Reason Why*, and by the film subsequently made from it, but by no means all the generals were as arrogant, stupid and inflexible as Cardigan and Lucan. The campaign was, in fact, conducted a good deal more successfully than Napoleon's war with Russia, or Hitler's for that matter. The British and their allies did not make the fatal mistake of marching on Moscow, but chose instead to fight the Russians in an area of their own choosing. Nor did they lose the war; the Russians ultimately asked for peace and abandoned their intrigues in the Middle East—for the time being at least. There was, of course, astonishing administrative incompetence, but this was a fact of military life at that time, due mainly to the view held by nearly all civilians that soldiers were expendable. The French suffered in similar fashion after Solferino and Magenta, as did the Federals and Confederates in the American Civil War. Nevertheless, there were many good officers and soldiers in the Crimea and the 33rd particularly distinguished themselves.

On September 20, 1854 they were the leading battalion of the leading brigade in the storming of the heights of the Alma, and in the space of three hours lost more killed and wounded than had been lost at Waterloo. After fording the river Alma they had to fight their way up to the heights, crowned by Russian entrenchments and well-sited batteries which poured an unceasing fire on the British infantry. The 33rd advanced as if on parade and lost 239 killed or wounded. No fewer than five officers and ten sergeants fell while carrying the Colours, and many died subsequently in the primitive hospitals. No other regiment taking part in the battle suffered so severely as the 33rd and their commanding officer, Lieutenant-Colonel Blake, was justly proud of his men. Again, at Inkerman on November 5, the Regiment

A private soldier of the 33rd Foot at the time of the Crimean War

stood firm in the drizzling rain as the Russian columns
loomed out of the fog and fought hand to hand with the
British infantry. Inkerman was a true 'soldiers' battle' and
in the end British tenacity triumphed over Russian courage.
The Russians withdrew, though the British were too ex-

hausted to follow them up. They settled down instead to the long siege of Sebastopol.

Those lucky enough to survive the winter of 1854–55 in the Crimea found it hard to forget. Little provision had been made for the Russian winter, either in clothing or in the construction of warm hutments. Men died like flies from exposure, scurvy, cholera and typhus. The sick rate was appalling and conditions in the hospitals became a national scandal. Only an army with superb morale and pride in regiment could have survived such trials, but the 33rd did so, and so did their comrades. Later, when the warmer weather came, they fought gallantly outside Sebastopol and contributed powerfully to its capture on September 8, 1855 by storming the Redan. But few who served in the Crimea were sorry when the campaign ended; there had been too much mismanagement, too much unnecessary suffering, and too little realization by the British people—until it was too late—of what the army was having to endure. The 33rd lost 14 officers and just under 1,000 men in the Crimea, more than half of whom died from disease or wounds. This was an appalling casualty list, but it did at least result in some long overdue reforms. The pity of it is that so many men had to die in order to prove the need.

There followed a short spell at home to recoup their strength and then the 33rd were off to India to take part in the operations in Central India to stamp out the embers of the Indian Mutiny. They were still in India in 1867 when the British government decided to send an expeditionary force to Abyssinia to punish King Theodore for imprisoning and maltreating British subjects in his capital at Magdala. The 33rd's commanding officer at this time was Lieutenant-Colonel Collings, but he was selected to command a Brigade and the Regiment was commanded by its second lieutenant-colonel, Alexander Dunn, who had won the V.C. when charging at Balaclava with the 11th Hussars. Dunn had eloped with his commanding officer's wife when he left the

Illustrated Times, 24th December 1858

Christmas Day in Barracks

11th Hussars, and after various adventures exchanged into the 33rd in 1864. A brother officer described him as a 'a tall, handsome man, 30 years of age . . . a kind, good-natured dandy, a bad commanding officer and not a good example to young officers . . . he was very popular but nearly destroyed the Regiment.' He was somewhat mysteriously killed in a shooting accident soon after landing in Abyssinia, but his short-comings as a commanding officer may account for the somewhat mixed reputation enjoyed by the 33rd during the campaign.

At the time the Regiment contained a large proportion of Irishmen—'hard drinkers all'.* They worked hard and were very smart but took every advantage of the soldier's privi-

* H. M. Stanley, the American journalist-explorer, who accompanied the expedition, described the 33rd as 'the Irish Regiment' in his book *To Magdala and Coomassie.*

lege to grouse. A staff officer who subsequently published his letters from Abyssinia severely criticizes the 33rd for this behaviour but they were exonerated by the historian of the campaign, Markham, who said of them, ' . . . if they could growl, they could also work—no man better.' And indeed they were required to work hard, constructing roads through solid rock with only picks and shovels, living on short rations, and marching 397 miles to Magdala and then back again. At all events their reputation must have been restored by the time they reached Magdala, since they were given the post of honour for the storm of Magdala, a rocky citadel high up on a mountain which King Theodore believed to be impregnable. The assault was rendered no easier by the fact that the Madras Sappers and Miners had omitted to bring with them the explosives to blow in the gate of the fortress, but the gallantry of Private Bergin and Drummer Magner found a way to penetrate the inner defences, an act which later earned them both the Victoria Cross, the first to be won by the 33rd. Soon the Regimental Colour was waving over the inner defences and Theodore's citadel was captured, the king committing suicide rather than surrender.* The 33rd brought back with them Theodore's throne cloth and also his shirt. They captured his silver drum as well, but Sir Robert Napier, who commanded the expeditionary force, ordered that it should be divided between the three British regiments taking part— the 4th (King's Own), 3rd Dragoon Guards, and the 33rd. In 1926, when the three regiments were together at Tidworth, the drum was reassembled and photographed. It was during this campaign that the Dukes first became connected with the Baluch Regiment; this is commemorated today by

* This was the last occasion when the 33rd carried their Colours in action. The storming party became separated during the assault which is the reason why only the Regimental Colour was waved above the main gate. The Queen's Colour was still outside with the main body of the stormers, much to the annoyance of Ensign Melliss who was carrying it. He was senior to Wynter who was carrying the Regimental Colour.

the regiment's affiliation with the 10th Battalion of the Baluch Regiment, Pakistan Army.

1881 was an important year for the 33rd and 76th. The old single battalion regiments were abolished and a system of

King Theodore's Drum

linked battalions was instituted, one at home matching another in foreign service. The new regiments were also formally affiliated to counties. Although the 33rd and 76th had little in common—other than the fact that they both wore scarlet facings and could claim to have had the name of Arthur Wesley inscribed on their muster rolls—it was decreed that they should be linked to form the First and Second Battalions of the Halifax Regiment (Duke of Wellington's), with headquarters at Halifax in the West Riding of Yorkshire. There was at first some confusion that the Halifax referred to might be Halifax in Canada and Colonel Allardice, then commanding the 76th in Ireland, and acting also on behalf of the 33rd who were in India, hastened to London to see the Commander-in-Chief. As a result of his petition the title was immediately altered to the Duke of Wellington's (West Riding Regiment); thereafter the regiment was always referred to officially as the West Riding Regiment until 1920 when the title was changed to the Duke of Wellington's Regiment (West Riding).

Although the Dukes' connection with Halifax is as much a source of pride today to the citizens as it is to the Regiment, it was not always thus. When first it was decided, in 1873, that a depot should be established at Halifax for the 33rd and 76th, a petition was signed by 4,664 of the townspeople protesting against the government's intention. They urged that military centres should be established only at a distance from towns, and especially from those involved in industry. It was argued that 'the temptation arising from frequent parades, reviews and other military spectacles offered inducements to irregularity and neglect of work;' and even worse was the prospect of 'the immorality and demoralization which all experience shows are the result of the congregation of large bodies of troops.' It must be remembered that these were the times of Kipling's poem, 'It's Tommy this, and Tommy that . . .' when 'to go for a soldier' was almost the last resort of a desperate man, but it is nevertheless pleasant to be able to record that the citizens soon came to accept the Dukes as *their* regiment, just as the Dukes have long since come to accept Halifax as *their* town.

It is equally pleasant to be able to report that the joining of the 33rd and 76th Regiments to form the Duke of Wellington's Regiment was attended with less recrimination and ill-feeling than was the case with many other regiments. Shot-gun marriages of this kind often give rise to problems, neither partner relishing the loss of its proud independence, and although the 1st and 2nd battalions still continued to refer to themselves as 33rd and 76th until their final amalgamation in 1948, both soon settled down to their new partnership. They seem most to have resented the loss of their scarlet facings, which had been changed for white in the reorganization of 1881, but scarlet facings were restored in 1905.

Chapter
5

South Africa and the Great War

THE next war in which the Dukes were engaged was the one fought in South Africa from 1899–1902 against the Boers. This has sometimes been described as 'the last of the gentlemen's wars', but there was certainly no inclination on the part of the Boers to pull their punches. They ran rings round the slow-moving and unimaginative British generals, provided an object lesson in the importance of weapon handling and marksmanship which, fortunately, the British Army was to take to heart, and managed to keep the war going for almost three years against what was then the most powerful country in the world. The early stages of the war, which produced disaster after disaster as far as the British were concerned, awakened the country to the short-comings of its military organization, and had almost as traumatic an effect on British public opinion as the events in the Crimea had done previously. This was fortunate, since it resulted in reforms which enabled the British Army to survive the far sterner tests of the early days of the Great War.

The 33rd arrived in Cape Town on January 20, 1900, thereby missing the blunders and disasters of the early days of the war. Lord Roberts had just arrived to take over as Commander-in-Chief and had brought with him Lord Kitchener as his Chief of Staff. The effect of this change of command can best be compared with the arrival of General Alexander to assume command in Cairo in August 1942, and with General Montgomery's assumption of the command of the Eighth Army at the same time. There was an immediate improvement in morale and in the organization of the campaign. The 33rd took part in the operations that relieved Kimberley and led to the surrender of Cronje, the senior Boer commander, at Paardeberg on February 28, 1900, the anniversary of Sir George Colley's defeat by the Boers at Majuba. They arrived on the battlefield on February 19, after marching throughout the previous day, and attacked across an open plain which was swept by enemy musketry. Few of the men had eaten for 24 hours and all of them were hungry. Nevertheless, the impetus of their attack caused Cronje to withdraw into his heavily-defended laager, where the Boers remained until his surrender. The 33rd lost 3 officers and 127 other ranks killed or wounded in the battle.

The Battle of Paardeberg resulted in the fall of Bloemfontein and the virtual over-running of the Orange Free State. There followed much hard marching across the veldt, for the Boers still had a good deal of fight left in them. At Rhenoster Kop on November 29, 1900, the 33rd lost their much-respected and popular commanding officer, Lieutenant-Colonel Lloyd, who was shot at a range of 180 yards and killed instantly.

Although it had been assumed that the surrender of President Kruger of the Transvaal after the occupation of Pretoria in September, 1900 would mark the end of the war, this did not turn out to be the case. The Boers continued in the field and, although there were no more pitched battles, there were numerous small engagements. Roberts returned home, leaving Kitchener to clean up the war, which took him nearly eighteen months and led to severe criticism of his policy of concentrating women and children in camps while sweeping areas clean of the Boer commandos. In the wide vistas of the veldt mobility was essential and large numbers of Mounted Infantry were required. The 76th, then stationed in Rangoon,* provided a company which

---

* The 76th lost all their regimental plate, both stands of Colours and many valuable pictures and books when the Officers' Mess was

remained in the field until the end of the war, and the 33rd also provided a company. The Boers were stout-hearted enemies, adept at the ambush and hit-and-run tactics, and weeks and weeks would pass in the pursuit of the elusive commandos. It was not the most exciting phase of the campaign, and casualties came more from disease than bullets, but it did at least teach the British Army some very important lessons—the use of ground, junior leadership, weapon handling and the importance of animal management. It is almost certainly as a result of the lessons so hardly learned in South Africa that the British Expeditionary Force which landed in France in August, 1914 was probably the best trained army we have ever sent to war.

When war was declared on Germany on August 4, 1914, the Duke of Wellington's Regiment consisted of two regular, one special reserve, and four territorial battalions. By the end of the war these seven battalions had been expanded to twenty-one and the Regiment had fought in France and Flanders, Gallipoli and Egypt, and in Italy. It had won 63 battle honours, 10 of which are emblazoned on the Colours, and had lost over 8,000 of all ranks. The 1st Battalion was in India throughout the war; it saw action on the North-West Frontier of India in 1919 in the Third Afghan War, winning the battle honour 'Afghanistan, 1919', but this was small consolation for missing action on the main fronts.

The 2nd Battalion, commanded by Lieutenant-Colonel Gibbs, was in Dublin when ordered to mobilize, and it embarked for France on August 13. It formed part of the 13th Brigade in General Fergusson's 5th Division, and the early morning of Sunday, August 23, 1914 saw the battalion deployed along the southern bank of the Condé Canal at St Ghislain, four miles west of Mons. The fog of war

---

burnt to the ground on December 20, 1901 at Rangoon. The elephant snuff-box presented by the Duke of Wellington and Lord Lake's dispatches were destroyed.

hung over Mons for most of that day, as Von Kluck's First Army bumped into the British Expeditionary Force and endeavoured to turn its flank and roll it up from the west. The superb musketry and fire discipline of the British Army succeeded in delaying the enemy advance, but the withdrawal of the French Fifth Army on the British right made retreat inevitable. Orders for the withdrawal were received on the night of August 23, and the Dukes, who had not been very heavily involved in the first day's fighting, now had to fall back through the maze of mining villages that lie between Mons and the French frontier. At one stage, around noon on August 24, the right flank of the Dukes was virtually in the air with the Germans rapidly working round them. Together with a battery of the 27th Brigade, Royal Field Artillery, the Battalion held the German advance for over an hour and a half, and when the Germans finally massed for the charge they were stopped dead in their tracks by the accurate marksmanship of the Dukes and the virtually point-blank fire of the Gunners. The Dukes had out-fought six German battalions, but they paid a heavy price; three officers had been killed, and seven wounded, including the commanding officer; two were missing. 40 other ranks were killed, 63 wounded, and 245 were missing. Compared with what came later these casualties were, of course, nothing exceptional, but coming as they did at the very outset of the campaign, and just before a long and trying withdrawal, it speaks volumes for the morale of the Battalion that it was not more seriously affected by these heavy losses.

There now followed the exhausting Retreat from Mons which was to last until September 5, with a brief pause at Le Cateau on August 26 when General Smith-Dorrien halted his II Corps and struck back at the advancing Germans.

'We took up a position in support of the Battalion and as an escort to the Battery,' wrote Lieutenant Ince. 'The remainder of the Battalion had taken up a position in trenches on the northern slope of the high ground south-west of Le Cateau.

The 26th was a beautiful day. The corn was lying on the ground in stooks, and during the night of August 25/26 we had been able to sleep out in the open in real comfort. . . . When the German attack commenced they were seen advancing on the slopes of Le Cateau and never shall I forget the 108th Battery shelling the German column at long range.'

The fighting began at dawn and continued throughout that stiflingly hot day. The brunt was born by the gallant Suffolks and Argyll and Sutherland Highlanders, most of whom died fighting, and the Dukes were lucky to escape with fairly light casualties, despite the heavy shelling. Orders were received for withdrawal at 2 p.m. and the Germans followed up closely until 6 p.m., when the pressure ceased. Meanwhile, the exhausted and thirsty Dukes stumbled back along the *pavé* until they reached Estrées, 15 miles south of Le Cateau, around midnight. There had been no rations issued on the two previous days, and the troops were utterly worn out by the time they had reached Estrées; and yet, by 2 a.m. on August 27, order had some-how been restored, and the Dukes marched off again at 4 a.m. in good fettle. It was a magnificent tribute to the training of the British Army and the pride in regiment which led men to give just that little more than they might other-wise have done.

The retreat continued in 'suffocating heat' until, on Sep-tember 6, the Dukes had reached the vicinity of Tournan.

'I remember,' wrote Lieutenant Ince, 'Sunday, September 6 was our turning-point and a red-letter day, as it was on this day that we received orders to turn round and advance against the enemy instead of continuing our retreat. I remember Captain Tidmarsh and I walking up to the top of some high ground near by and having a glimpse of Paris some 15 kilometres to the south-west of us. We had an excellent view of the Eiffel Tower and the dome of Notre Dame. I think it struck us some-what forcibly then as to the distance we had covered since Mons in so short a time, and the fact we had approached so near Paris. At 12 noon, on the 6th, we had a Church Parade in the square of Villeneuve, and in the afternoon we moved off in pursuit of the enemy. You can imagine the moral effect on us all of having the enemy *on the run* after our run of several days. We all felt as fit as ever and began to think the war was near its end. False hopes, I'm afraid.'

The Dukes had marched over 200 miles in 13 days, with only one short halt. Their ranks were full of reservists who were certainly not fighting fit when they arrived in France, and they had been forced to carry out an exhausting retreat, short of food and sleep, during one of the hottest Augusts in living memory. Yet all ranks went forward with a great surge of hope when Sir John French issued his orders on September 6 for the advance. The situation had been changed by Von Kluck's decision to wheel his army north of Paris, instead of encircling the city, and by Joffre's offensive against Von Bulow's army on the Marne. The battle of the Marne, which forced the Germans to withdraw behind the Aisne, was a series of disconnected engagements which are difficult to describe, but it was certainly the most decisive moment in the war. Although it was not appreciated at the time, the battle of the Marne, fought from September 6–14, prevented the Germans from winning the war, and should therefore be regarded as one of the Regiment's most cherished battle honours.

The advance was checked on the River Aisne, along the banks of which the Germans dug in and from where they resisted all attempts to evict them. There now began the 'race to the sea', both the Allies and the Germans vainly trying to outflank each other until the trenches reached Nieuport in October, 1914. The war of manoeuvre was over and henceforward artillery, barbed wire and the machine gun would dominate the battlefield. The generals of both sides, whose training had never envisaged such a situation, tried to smash their way through—'but in vain: they knew not the answer and merely destroyed more lives.'* Tens of

* *A History of Warfare* by Field-Marshal Viscount Montgomery (Collins) 1968.

thousands of lives were sacrificed to gain or defend a few square miles of blood-soaked ground. This self-sacrifice, almost beyond our comprehension today, is commemorated by the crosses standing rank upon rank in the war cemeteries of France and Flanders, and for every man whose last resting place is marked, there is probably another who has no memorial. It is impossible to visit these cemeteries without feeling both pity and pride—pity for the horror of it all, and pride that men could endure so much.

As the line of trenches extended across northern France, the Dukes moved steadily nearer Ypres in Flanders, by marching along the *pavé*, and by train. The first Battle of Ypres began on October 19, with the German attempt to break through the thin British line and drive on to the sea, and ended on November 22, by which time the entire British Expeditionary Force had truly been hammered on the anvil, and yet still survived.

> 'It was on' November 5, 1914, that the Dukes got their first sight of the beautiful old Town Hall, and during the remainder of that month and drenching wet put in some as severe fighting as occurred during the whole course of the war. The day-to-day happenings of these nerve-racking days is more or less simple to record. The ceaseless strain both physical and mental of such fighting is best left to the imagination of the reader.'[*]

In fact, it is hard for later generations to imagine the conditions which existed in the Ypres Salient. Colonel Harrison, who commanded the 2nd Battalion at Ypres, wrote in his diary for Wednesday, November 4, 1914:

> 'Orders came to march to Ypres tomorrow to join the I Corps. We were here 15 officers and 800 rank and file. I tried my best to get hold of a photographer at Bailleul so as to have an officers' group taken, we also had two officers on the staff to add to this number; unfortunately orders came to move before it could be done. *Less than three weeks later we were 2 officers and 380 men.*' [Author's italics].

[*] *History of the Duke of Wellington's Regiment 1881–1923* by Brigadier-General C. D. Bruce (Medici Society) 1927.

Hill 60—April 1915

From then until the end of the war the old 76th was constantly in and out of action. At Hill 60, on April 18 and May 5, 1915 the Battalion was bled white, first to take, and then to hold, a nondescript bump rising a bare 50 feet above the Flanders plain, which measured about 250 yards long by 200 wide. Here, between April 17 and 21, the Dukes fought and died under the hail of a virtually ceaseless artillery bombardment. In those four days they lost 15 officers and 363 rank and file killed or wounded, with 43 missing. Later, on May 5, after a short rest, they were back on Hill 60 when the Germans counter-attacked, using chlorine gas. There were no gas masks and men therefore stood at their posts and were choked to death. The Dukes suffered over 300 casualties that morning, but they still managed to hang on to the reserve trenches. None of the Regiment's battle honours has been more hardly won than 'Hill 60.'

The next holocaust was to be on the Somme, where the battle lasted from July 1 to November 18, 1916. During this

1/5 Battalion in the trenches at Ypres, winter, 1915

period the casualties were about equal—500,000 on both sides killed, wounded, or taken prisoner. The 2nd Battalion was involved in the fighting and suffered heavy casualties, and by this time they had been joined in France by other battalions of the Regiment, both Territorial and 'Service' battalions raised only for the period of the war. No less than nine battalions of the Dukes took part in the Battle of the Somme, and by this stage of the war there was little to differentiate a battalion of the pre-1914 Regular Army from a battalion of the New Army. All displayed equal gallantry and all were immensely proud of the traditions of the Regiment. Five V.C.s had been awarded to members of the Regiment by the end of the war, and all of these went to Territorial or 'Service' battalions.★

The 8th Battalion fought at Gallipoli, and also in Egypt and France. The 10th Battalion fought in Italy, as well as in

★ Victoria Crosses were awarded to 2/Lieutenant H. Kelly, 10th Battalion: Private A. Loosemore, 8th Battalion: Private A. Poulter, 1/4th Battalion: Private H. Tandey, D.C.M., M.M., and 2/Lieutenant J. P. Huffam, both of the 5th Battalion.

France; the 2nd Battalion went back to Ypres after taking part in the Battle of Arras in April, 1917. They lost their commanding officer, Lieutenant-Colonel Horsfall, at Passchendaele, and 169 officers and men besides. There the enemy was as much the mud and severe climatic conditions as it was Germans, and Haig has been severely criticized for persisting with his offensive when the prospects of success were clearly nil.

When hostilities ceased on November 11, 1918, the 2nd Battalion was billeted not far from Valenciennes, less than 20 miles from Mons where they had started the campaign. It had been a long, hard war, quite unlike anything anticipated when the Battalion embarked at Dublin four years previously. The toll of lives had been tragic, but morale had remained high throughout. This was not only a tribute to Yorkshire character but also to the regimental tradition which held men together—even when they had come very near to the breaking point.

Chapter
6

The Second World War

THE many people who thought that the Great War of 1914–1918 would be the 'war to end all wars', were soon to have their hopes shattered. However, the signing of the Peace Treaty at Versailles provided an admirable excuse to reduce defence expenditure, and it was Winston Churchill, when Chancellor of Exchequer, who directed his officials to work on the principle of 'no war for ten years' when scrutinizing the Services' estimates. The Services were, in consequence, starved of money; the Dukes, in common with the rest of the Army, suffered from this short-sighted policy. Recruiting fell off, which meant that battalions on the home establishment were usually well below strength. Promotion was slow (subalterns of 15 and 16 years' service were not uncommon), and equipment was so short that coloured flags were carried on manœuvres to represent anti-tank guns. It is indeed surprising that, despite these frustrations, the British Army was able to produce generals like Wavell, Alexander and Montgomery, and the Indian Army generals like Auchinleck and Slim, when war came.

The 1st Battalion moved from India to Palestine in 1920, and later returned home. In 1923 it was sent to Constantinople and was involved in the Chanak incident, where we found ourselves in a face-to-face confrontation with the Turks, fresh from their victory over the Greeks and bursting with nationalistic fervour. The diplomacy of the British commander, General Harington, was successful in avoiding an armed clash, which could have led to war, and the 33rd returned home towards the end of the year. It remained on the home establishment for most of the intervening years until the outbreak of the Second World War, except from 1935–1937 when it was in Malta. While in Malta the Battalion was joined by 2/Lieutenant the Earl of Mornington, better known as 'Morny,' eldest son of the 5th Duke and a direct descendent of the Duke of Wellington. 'Morny' used to say that his ambition was to be Lieutenant-Colonel the Duke of Wellington commanding the Duke of Wellington's Regiment, but this was not to be. He seconded to the King's African Rifles in 1939 and saw service with them in Abyssinia. On returning to England in 1942 he joined the Commandos and was killed at Salerno in September 1943. He had succeeded as 6th Duke of Wellington in 1941.

The 2nd Battalion served in Ireland, Egypt, Singapore and India between the wars, and in 1934 took part in the Looe Agra operations on the North-West Frontier of India. The commanding officer at that time was Lieutenant-Colonel Cox, who had embarked for France with the battalion in 1914. The Adjutant, a little later on, was Lieutenant Bray,* whose father had commanded the 76th with great distinction during the battle of the Somme in 1916. The Looe Agra operations involved a great deal of marching, as well as the exhausting business of picqueting the hills—2,000 feet or more—as the column moved along the valleys. There was also a great deal of sniping. By the time the operations were over the Dukes had become expert in the somewhat specialized requirements of mountain warfare, and this was as well, because the following year they were involved in the Mohmand operations.

The Mohmand operations did not differ from other North-West Frontier operations but are interesting because the two Brigade Commanders involved, Auchinleck commanding

---

* Now General Sir Robert Bray, recently Deputy Supreme Allied Commander Europe (1967–1970) and Colonel of the Duke of Wellington's Regiment.

The 6th Duke of Wellington; killed at Salerno, September, 1943

the Peshawar Brigade, and Alexander commanding the Nowshera Brigade (which included the Dukes), were soon to achieve fame and reach high rank in the Second World War. It was during these operations that the Guides Infantry, an Indian Army unit with a well deserved reputation on the North-West Frontier, became involved in hand-to-hand fighting with the tribesmen, as a result of which Major Meynell received the posthumous award of the V.C. The course of the battle could easily be observed from Regimental Headquarters of the Dukes, but the Battalion was too far away to be able to intervene in the battle.

When war was declared on September 3, 1939 the 1st Battalion was at Bordon, and the 2nd Battalion was at Multan in India. It seemed likely at the time that the roles of the two battalions during the Great War were going to be reversed, the 33rd seeing all the action, while the 76th remained on garrison duty in India. No-one then envisaged that the war would spread until even remote atolls in the South Pacific became the scene of fierce fighting.

The Territorial Army suffered even more between the wars than the Regular Army from the demand for economy. It was re-formed in 1919 and at the time the regiment had four territorial battalions—4th (Halifax), 5th (Huddersfield), 6th (Skipton), and 7th (Milnsbridge). These battalions formed the 147th (2nd West Riding) Infantry Brigade, but in 1936 certain changes were made in order to provide more effective defence against air attacks on the country. The 5th Battalion was converted to a searchlight battalion, R.E. Two years later the 4th Battalion became an anti-tank regiment R.A. In the spring of 1939 the Territorial Army was doubled, making up in numbers what it woefully lacked in training and equipment. At the outbreak of war the 1/6th, 2/6th, 1/7th, and 2/7th were the Territorial infantry battalions of the Duke of Wellington's Regiment. Later the 8th, 9th and 10th battalions were re-raised, the two former becoming R.A.C. regiments, while the 10th remained at home and fulfilled a variety of training roles.*

The 33rd went overseas in September, 1939 as part of the 1st Division in the B.E.F. It was commanded by Lieutenant-Colonel (later Major-General) Beard. There followed eight months of inactivity, since described as the 'phoney war', spent mainly in digging defences to extend the Maginot Line. 'As it was forbidden to cut the French crops to gain fields of fire, the defences had to be built up in the form of breastworks' †—a typical example of the difficulties of that time. The Dukes can, however, claim to have been the first British troops to cross into enemy territory; this was a listening patrol led by Lieutenant Bucknall.

The 'phoney war' came to an end on May 10, 1940 when the Germans invaded Holland and Belgium. The 33rd moved forward into Belgium and were digging-in on the outskirts of Brussels when the orders came to withdraw. There was considerable confusion as the B.E.F. fell back to conform with the movements of the Belgians and the French. At one stage the Dukes found themselves at Lille, and at another in Armentières, before the order was received for the Battalion to fall back on Dunkirk for evacuation to England. They formed part of the rear guard, and their gallant and stubborn defence played an important part in enabling the greater part of the B.E.F. to be evacuated. A letter received subsequently by the Colonel of the Regiment‡ from Brigadier Wilson, commanding the 3rd Infantry Brigade, pays tribute to the 33rd's conduct during those difficult and dark days:

* 1/4th became 58th Anti-Tank Regiment R.A. (4th D.W.R.).
2/4th became 68th Anti-Tank Regiment R.A. (2/4th D.W.R.)
5th eventually became 43rd Searchlight Regiment, R.A.
8th became 145th Regiment, Royal Armoured Corps.
9th became 146th Regiment, Royal Armoured Corps.
† *The History of the Duke of Wellington's Regiment 1919-1952* by Brigadier C. N. Barclay (Clowes 1953)
‡ Colonel C. J. Pickering, commanded 2nd Battalion 1925–29; Colonel of the Regiment 1938–47.

I am very proud to have had the privilege of having under my command such a magnificent battalion as the 1st Battalion of your Regiment. During the recent operations their fighting efficiency and stubborn determination were in keeping with the highest traditions of the past. The Battalion was in close contact with the enemy from the commencement of the operations until embarkation at Dunkirk. They never once gave ground unless ordered to do so, and on more than one occasion inflicted severe losses on the enemy. The steadiness of all ranks under heavy enemy fire, sometimes in very exposed positions, was exemplary. I would particularly mention the defence of the final bridgehead in front of Dunkirk. The Battalion was ordered to hold a very extended and exposed position. For the last 48 hours they were subjected to constant and heavy enemy pressure. No reserves were available. It was essential for the safety of the force as a whole that this position should be maintained intact until the final withdrawal took place. The Battalion succeeded in this difficult task as a result of first-class leadership and the courage and determination of all ranks. They then carried out a successful withdrawal when still in close contact and still under pressure.

Although wars are not won by withdrawals, as Winston Churchill was quick to point out to the House of Commons after Dunkirk, retreats probably make higher demands on the soldier than any other operation of war. The 33rd had come through the test with flying colours, as the 76th were later to do in Burma, but mention must also be made of the 2/6th and 2/7th Battalions, which were also involved in operations in France in 1940. Both these battalions had been newly formed and were short of equipment and training; they were intended to perform pioneering duties in the rear areas of the B.E.F. and then only for a few months. Instead they were sucked into the maelstrom and required to stem the onrush of the German Panzer divisions. It would be hard to describe in a few words the chaotic conditions which prevailed in France at that time, but both the 2/6th and 2/7th put up a gallant resistance before they were finally evacuated.

The next withdrawal in which the Dukes were involved

Imperial War Museum

The River Sittang, Burma, 1942

took place in Burma during the first six months of 1942. The 2nd Battalion, then stationed in Peshawar, landed at Rangoon on February 14, 1942, and were almost immediately sent forward to join 17th Indian Division, which was withdrawing under severe enemy pressure towards the River Sittang. This river was the last natural obstacle between the Japanese and Rangoon, and was crossed by only one bridge at Mokpalin. It was a railway bridge and had to be prepared by the Sappers before it could take wheeled transport. Time was needed to do this but the Japanese worked round the flanks of the Division and penetrated the defences of the bridgehead. Much of the fighting took place in thick jungle, and in darkness, and at one stage it seemed certain that the bridge would be lost to the enemy. The decision was therefore made to destroy it, and it was in fact blown in the early hours of February 24, leaving the greater part of 17th Division on the wrong side of the obstacle.

The following eyewitness account of the Battle of the Sittang gives some idea of what the Battalion went through:

Sittang was our first taste of the Japanese and was a real 'soldiers' battle' The Japs, following their usual tactics, had cut round behind us and our Brigade, the 46th, was ambushed on the line of march, while still some distance from the bridge. The transport, which had moved back earlier, met a similar fate. They received a message, afterwards thought to be false, which instructed them to pull in and halt, and were ambushed in their trucks. The resistance they put up was magnificent and Pte. Rawnsley of B Company earned his M.M. in this action. Later the same night (23rd February) Sittang Bridge was blown with over two Brigades still the wrong side of the river, and the Battalion, which had become rather scattered, had a very unpleasant night. Firing was going on continuously and next morning they were bombed and mortared.

At various times next day the Battalion got across the river. The swim was about 800 yards and the scene on the bank would have made a fortune of any film producer. Rafts were made for the wounded, and kit and equipment, including arms, littered the bank. Those who could swim assisted the non-swimmers. Many non-swimmers determined to make a fight of it and have never been seen again. A bedraggled Battalion with little uniform except under-pants, finally arrived at the far bank where D Company, under Donald Coningham, had been left to hold the bridgehead. B Company were divorced from the Battalion and made their way around behind the Sittang, and were finally rowed across by the Burmese some six to eight miles north of the bridge, and arrived back at Pegu where the Battalion was re-forming and re-equipping. The first person the author saw was Bob Moran clad picturesquely but simply in vest, long shorts and a canvas water bucket in lieu of a topee.

Many gallant deeds were done that day, and none more gallant than those of Major Robinson, commanding C Company, who organized the escape across the river of over 500 Gurkha and Indian troops, besides his own Company. The Dukes lost their commanding officer, Lieutenant-Colonel Owen, at the Sittang. He managed to swim the river but was murdered by dacoits while resting in a village hut.

The decision whether or not to blow a bridge is probably the hardest any commander has to take, and there will always be controversy over the blowing of the Sittang Bridge. It has been further complicated by the fact that the Japanese eased their pressure on the bridgehead once they knew the bridge was blown, thus enabling quite considerable numbers of troops to escape. Had the bridge remained intact, they almost certainly would have maintained their pressure and would probably have succeeded in capturing the bridge. As it was, the 76th lived to fight another day, but it was a battered battalion which re-formed at Pegu after suffering over 100 casualties* at the Sittang. Thereafter the 76th took part in the long withdrawal through Burma which ended with their arrival at Imphal on May 22, 1942. They had marched over 700 miles as the crow flies, fought numerous engagements with the Japanese, and had successfully survived the disaster at the Sittang. For this much credit is due to their commanding officer for much of the retreat, Lieutenant-Colonel Faithfull, whose complete disregard for his own safety was an inspiration to all ranks.

Fortunately there were to be no more withdrawals for the Dukes. The 1st Battalion embarked at Avonmouth on February 26, 1943 to join the First Army in Tunisia. There it gained great distinction by its gallant defence of Banana Ridge and Point 174 from April 19 to 22, thereby protecting the concentration of First Army artillery which was being deployed in the basin behind them. The 33rd were unable to dig trenches on the ridge for fear of alarming the enemy, and as a result, when the Germans launched a fierce attack to spoil the impending First Army assault, the Dukes had to fight it out in the open with the enemy tanks milling around them. But fight it out they did, supported by tanks of the 145th Regiment R.A.C., which had begun its existence as the 8th Dukes, and Banana Ridge was held intact. The staunchness of the Dukes in their first real battle in North Africa enabled the First Army attack to go in as planned.

* A large number were drowned trying to swim the fast-flowing river.

The 33rd took part in this attack which was delivered by the 1st and 4th Divisions, but not until they had been rested after their battle on Banana Ridge. They were then required to assault and capture Djebel Bou Aoukaz, a feature dominating the Medjez-el-Bab/Tunis road, which had held up the 24th Guards Brigade. The 33rd, in company with the K.S.L.I. and Sherwood Foresters, fought a fierce battle on May 5 and 6 which ended in the capture of the Djebel at the cost of 111 casualties. The way to Tunis now lay open and the armour passed through; 'The Dukes—literally bloody but unbowed—were master of the Bou and the fall of the Axis in North Africa was inevitable,' wrote the 33rd's commanding officer, Lieutenant-Colonel Webb-Carter, who received the immediate award of the D.S.O. for his gallantry and leadership, and who subsequently had the honour of leading the 3rd Infantry Brigade representatives in the Victory Parade in Tunis.

The next operation was the capture of Pantellaria Island, which at first seemed to be a tougher operation than it eventually turned out to be. The Italian garrison had no stomach for the fight and surrendered after bombardment from the sea and air. The 1st Battalion then returned to North Africa where they spent five months training hard for their next battle, which was to be in Italy. It was to turn out to be one of the hardest-fought battles in all the 33rd's long history.

The 33rd moved to Italy early in December, 1943. The Allies had by now occupied most of southern Italy but were held up in the mountains north of Naples. The next objective was Rome and it was planned to capture Anzio by amphibious assault and the advance on Rome in combination with an advance on the main battle front. The amphibious force consisted of British and American formations, and the Dukes landed at Anzio on the morning of January 23, 1944. The Germans had been taken by surprise and there was little real opposition to the landing. The way to

Rome seemed open but the Allied commander took counsel of his fears, and in any case omitted to take into consideration the quick reactions of the German high command when confronted with a situation of this kind. The Germans certainly reacted with astonishing speed at a time when the Allies were probing cautiously forward. Scraping together any troops on which he could lay his hands, Field-Marshal Kesselring, the German commander in Italy, hastily plugged the gaps in his defences. Soon the 33rd was engaged in fierce fighting to retain the beach-head. Within ten days of the landing, elements of some four German divisions were counter-attacking, supported by heavy tanks and artillery.

The battle now degenerated into a form of trench warfare with the Germans endeavouring to drive the Allies into the sea, while the Allies held on by their eyebrows. The 33rd

Imperial War Museum

The Anzio Beach-head, January 1944

Imperial War Museum

The 1st Battalion marching past General Mark Clark, Rome, June, 1944

fought with its accustomed staunchness, but at a heavy cost. They lost particularly heavily when holding the sector known as the Wadis, of which the commanding officer wrote:

> The bringing up of supplies was a recurrent nightmare. Carrying parties got lost; jeeps got bogged, and then, as the cursing troops heaved at them, down would come the mortar shells . . . Some stupendous things were done by all ranks . . . Almost imperceptibly the situation improved. Our patrols gradually gained ascendancy, our snipers made the enemy cautious, and through it all the indomitable courage of the British private soldier shone as ever. The Wadis. No soldier of the 1st Division who fought at Anzio will ever forget them.

The 33rd lost 39 officers and 921 other ranks during the Anzio operation, and this represents nearly 11 per cent of the total casualties suffered by the 1st Division. When finally the break-through came at the end of May, the Battalion was selected to represent the British Army in the formal entry into Rome. The salute was taken by General Mark Clark, the American general commanding the Fifth Army, and for a short period the 33rd formed part of the Rome garrison. In the words of the Regimental History—

> thus ended the campaign of the Anzio beach-head, a campaign which was won, not by great decisions at high level, but by the courage and skill of regimental officers and men. The Dukes gained much glory, but the price was a heavy one.

It will probably be convenient to complete the story of the 33rd in Italy before turning to the other battalions. After the fall of Rome there was a hard and bitter slogging match as the Germans fought desperately to hold their mountain redoubt while the Allies tried to break through into the Po Valley. Unfortunately, Field-Marshal Alexander's Army Group had been greatly weakened by the requirement to provide troops for the landing in the south of France, and complete victory in Italy, which at one time had seemed almost imminent, became increasingly deferred. Some of the toughest fighting of the entire campaign followed the fall of Rome, as the Allies fought their way into the Apennines. It was during this fighting, at Mt. Ceco on October 8, 1944, that Private R. Burton of A Company won the Victoria Cross for magnificent gallantry. On the same day the 33rd lost their commanding officer, Lieutenant-Colonel Shiel, who was mortally wounded; he had succeeded Lieutenant-Colonel Webb-Carter the previous September. By Christmas Day heavy snowfalls had slowed down operations in the mountains to patrol activities, and early in 1945 the 1st Division, and with it the 33rd, were moved to Palestine. They were in camp at Haifa on May 8 when the war against Germany ended. Both in North Africa and in Italy the 33rd had been in the thick of the fighting and had acquitted themselves in the best traditions of the regiment.

The 76th, after their long and arduous withdrawal from Burma, were re-equipped as a Support Battalion. They were completely mechanized, with carriers and jeeps, and lavishly provided with Bren guns. However, the success of Brigadier (later Major-General) Wingate's deep penetration into Burma with his Chindit columns during the dry season of 1943 led to the expansion of Wingate's force, and the 76th was one of the units selected for this exacting role. Mechanized operations gave way to training to survive in the jungle under the most arduous physical conditions. Wingate insisted that every man should be able to march 90 miles through the jungle carrying a 60 pound pack, his weapons and ammunition. Supply was by air-drop, and river crossing was an essential part of the training—as was animal management. It was intended to launch these Chindit operations into Burma early in 1944, one brigade marching into Burma while the other three brigades were to be flown in by gliders and Dakotas. Although, in fact, the first part of the operation went according to plan, its further development was forestalled by the Japanese offensive against Imphal. The 23rd Brigade, the only Chindit brigade not

Imperial War Museum

1/7th Battalion attacking in Holland, January, 1945

A 9th Battalion tank at Ramree Island, January, 1945

committed (which included the 2nd Battalion), was given the task of severing the Japanese lines of communication with Burma. The battalion provided two columns, the 33rd and 76th, each consisting of some 400 officers and men, 70 mules, 12 chargers and 12 bullocks. From the beginning of April until the end of July, 1944 these columns operated against the Japanese in the thickly jungle-covered Naga Hills, some of the most difficult terrain in the world, for much of the time during the torrential monsoon, and in areas where tick typhus and cerebral malaria is endemic. They were completely successful in their task of interfering with, and finally severing, the Japanese communications, and proved conclusively that the British soldier, when properly trained, was just as tough a jungle fighter as the Japanese. By the end of the operations nearly half the

Battalion were in hospital with wounds, disease or malnutrition, but the retreat of 1942 had been amply avenged. The 76th then moved to Dehra Dun to recuperate and train, and it was there they celebrated V.J. Day.

The 1/6th and 1/7th Battalions took part in the Normandy Landing in 1944, but the former had, unfortunately, to be broken up in August, after suffering heavy casualties, to provide reinforcements for the 1/7th. The 1/7th enjoyed a great reputation in the 49th Division, fighting with great skill and gallantry in the *bocage* and then in the capture of Le Havre. It took part in the advance into the Low Countries and was involved in the liberation of northern Holland. The 8th Battalion, subsequently re-numbered 145th Regiment, R.A.C., fought in Italy. The 9th Battalion, re-numbered 146th Regiment, R.A.C., served in India, and later took part in operations in the Arakan, on Ramree Island, and in Sumatra after the Japanese surrender. The Dukes can therefore claim to have been represented in all the main theatres of war in which British troops were engaged, with the exception of the Middle East and the Pacific, and when the war ended ten new battle honours were added to the Colours.

Chapter
7
'The Hook'

WHEN THE war ended the 33rd were in Palestine and the 76th were in India. The 33rd were involved in the unpleasant task of Internal Security at a time when illegal Jewish immigration was enormously complicating an already apparently insoluble problem; it was therefore a relief when they moved to Khartoum in December, 1946. The 76th were in Meerut, one of the largest military cantonments in India, and on New Year's Day, 1947 the battalion paraded for the first time since 1940 with its two stands of Colours. Only the commanding officer, Lieutenant-Colonel Armitage, and one N.C.O.—a late Mess Sergeant—had ever seen the Colours before. It was in a way symbolic that the Honorary Colours, presented nearly 150 years before to mark the 76th's part in the conquest of India, should have been paraded at the beginning of 1947—the year India became independent. Fortunately the 76th were spared involvement in the ghastly blood-bath that ushered in independence, sailing from India on September 19, 1947, but, as seems entirely appropriate, the old 76th 'Hindustan' Regiment of Foot was the last British unit to render a Royal Salute to a Viceroy of India, on August 15, 1947.

The 76th arrived home to be amalgamated with the 33rd, returned from the Sudan a few months previously. As part of the reduction in the strength of the Army it had been decided that most of the two-battalion Regiments of the Line would be reduced to one battalion by amalgamation, and on June 17, 1948 the amalgamation parade was held at

The late Earl of Scarborough, General Sir Philip Christison, the Duke of Wellington and the Mayor of Halifax outside the Depot Mess, 1952

Strensall, in the course of which the Colonel of the Regiment, General Sir Philip Christison,* formally handed over the 2nd Battalion's two stands of Colours to the 1st Battalion. Thus ended the independent existence of two old and distinguished battalions which had endured so much danger and hardship, and won so much glory. The amalgamated battalion which had the responsibility of perpetuating a great tradition was soon to prove that it was in every way worthy of its trust.

* General Sir Philip Christison, Bart., commanded the 2nd Battalion in 1937–38 and was Colonel of the Regiment from 1947–1957. He had the unique distinction of earning the D.S.O. as a lieutenant-general for personal leadership after being knighted in the field. His only son, John, was killed in action in Burma with the 2nd Battalion in March, 1942.

In 1945, on the 130th anniversary of the Battle of Waterloo, the long and valued connection of the Dukes with Halifax had been further strengthened by the grant to the Regiment of the Freedom of the Borough, and on July 2, 1952, the Regiment was similarly honoured by the grant of the Freedom of Huddersfield. This close connection with the West Riding had been reinforced by the re-formation of the Territorial Army in 1947. The 7th Battalion, with headquarters at Milnsbridge, was restored to the establishment, but unfortunately has since been disbanded as a result of the virtual dissolution of the Territorial Army.

At the end of September, 1952, the 1st Battalion, commanded by Lieutenant-Colonel Bunbury, sailed for Korea to join the Commonwealth Division, as part of the United

Imperial War Museum

The Hook, Korea, 1953

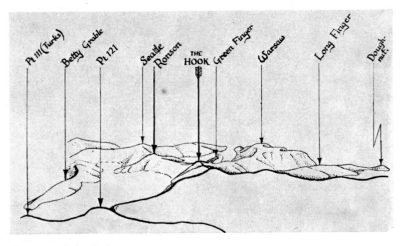

Panorama of the Hook

Nations Forces. Throughout that bitter Korean winter the Dukes distinguished themselves by their efficient and aggressive patrolling and by their high morale. In the middle of May, 1953 the Battalion found itself garrisoning 'The Hook', a prominent hill feature on the left of the Commonwealth Division sector. 'The Hook' was of great tactical importance and it had been known for some time that the Chinese intended to capture it. On the night of May 7/8 they had launched an attack on the 1st Battalion, the Black Watch, who were then holding 'The Hook,' but had been driven off with some loss. The Dukes relieved the Black Watch on May 13. The actual Hook feature is a hill forming a rifle company position in the centre of the left-hand battalion sector. The sector is shaped like a horse-shoe based on four prominent hill features, and this fact necessitated the loan of a rifle company from the reserve battalion [of the Brigade] in order that the 'Hook Battalion' could have its own reserve company sited tactically and in depth.

The Soldier

Incident in the Battle of the Hook, 28th May 1953

The terrain was such that the enemy could make use of 'dead ground' to infiltrate very close to the Dukes' defences, and prior to the battle the Chinese were successful in doing this, digging themselves bomb-proof dug-outs in the steep hillsides despite the defensive fire put down by the Battalion's mortars and the supporting artillery. Indeed it was so obvious that the Chinese intended to launch a major attack that from the moment the Dukes arrived on 'The Hook' not a minute was lost in improving the defences by strengthening bunkers, deepening communication trenches, and laying additional wire to block possible avenues of approach.

Enemy shelling began on the night of May 26/27, the guns being of heavy calibre and carefully registered. Suddenly, at 1953 hours, the main Chinese artillery and mortar concentration descended on 'The Hook', the chief weight falling on the forward platoon. The enemy barrage was followed by the first wave of infantry, which overran the forward platoon. The platoon commander, 2/Lieutenant Kirk, was killed in the fierce hand-to-hand fighting that followed, and soon any kind of coordinated platoon action became impossible. Fighting in the best tradition of the Dukes, the survivors of the platoon were forced back into shelter tunnels, which they continued to defend until the entrances were blown in by the Chinese with satchel charges. Simultaneously three separate waves of the enemy attacked 'The Hook' from the Ronson spur, but were scattered by artillery and L.M.G. fire. Other Chinese attacks were held up by the wire, and within thirty minutes of the battle starting two enemy companies had been virtually wiped out.

The Chinese were determined to take 'The Hook' and were undeterred by their initial casualties. They increased their artillery and mortar fire and attacked again at 2045 hours, penetrating the right-hand platoon position but suffering heavy casualties. The gap was plugged and another

Chinese company was caught by artillery as it was forming-up and decimated. Further attacks followed, including one of battalion strength which suffered such appalling casualties from the defensive fire of the Divisional artillery that it never left its start-line. The final attack took place at 0030 hours on May 27 but was broken up by the fire of the Assault Pioneer Platoon, supported by tank fire, as well as by mortars and artillery. Thirty enemy dead were counted on the wire the following morning.

Meanwhile the enemy had to be evicted from such foot-holds as they might have gained on 'The Hook'. A careful plan had been made for this operation; it began at 2330 hours, and by 0430 hours Lieutenant-Colonel Bunbury was able to report that 'The Hook' was clear of the enemy. It was subsequently established that no less than eight Chinese companies from three battalions, specially trained, were involved in the attack; their estimated casualties were 250 killed and over 800 wounded, representing a casualty figure of 65 per cent of the troops involved. The price paid by the Dukes for their gallant defence of 'The Hook' was 32 dead and 5 missing, but in the words of their Brigade Commander (Brigadier, later Major-General, Kendrew): 'The Dukes did what I told them. They held the Hook.'

'The Hook, 1953' has now been added to the Regiment's long list of battle honours, but the Dukes would be the first to admit that it was a battle won as a result of the cooperation of all Arms. They would certainly wish to pay tribute to the support they received from the 1st Royal Tank Regiment, 20th Field Regiment, Royal Artillery, the King's Regiment, and of course to the Divisional Artillery as a whole.

Since their return from Korea the Regiment has experienced to the full the 'turbulence' which has been the lot of the British soldier since the Second World War ended in 1945. The Dukes have served in Gibraltar, Malta, Cyprus, Kenya, Northern Ireland, Germany and, at irregular

1st Battalion patrol, Hong Kong, 1969

intervals, in England. They were involved in the arduous
internal security operations in Cyprus during which they
successfully dealt with several terrorists, including the
notorious Afxentiou Group. They have recently been
stationed in Hong Kong. Wherever they have served, they
have shown themselves to be as dependable in barracks and
in the field as they have been redoubtable on the rifle range
and at sport. They still bear the name of the Duke in their
title and in 1969 were allowed to revert to their former cap
badge, the crest of the Duke of Wellington on a scroll bear-
ing the words 'The West Riding'.

Epilogue

Yorkshiremen are not much given to boasting about their prowess; they are inclined on the whole to be taciturn and prefer deeds to words. If, however, an exception has to be made to this general rule, it will relate to sport. Every Yorkshireman knows that Yorkshire plays the best cricket, trains the best horses, and in Leeds United possesses one of the best football sides in the country. He probably also knows that the record of the Dukes on the rugby field may have been equalled on occasions, but has certainly never been excelled since organized sport came to be recognized as an essential part of the training of the British soldier. For this reason no account of the Duke of Wellington's Regiment can possibly be written without some reference being made to the Dukes' rugby record.

Beginning in 1895, when the 2nd Battalion won the Natal Rugby Cup in South Africa for three years running, the Dukes have always been in the first flight of Army rugby sides. The 1st Battalion won the coveted Calcutta Cup in India for eight years in succession before the Great War; the 2nd Battalion won the All India Championship in 1937, and were runners up in 1930, 1933 and 1934. The Army Cup has been won nine times by the Regiment; in 1907, 1914, 1931, 1933, 1958 and 1964–68, and they were runners up in 1960 and 1961. When they were stationed in Northern Ireland from 1957–1959 the Dukes played all the first-class Irish Clubs' sides, including Queen's University and Trinity College, Dublin, and recorded victories against most of them. So impressive was their record that Ulster

1st Battalion Rugby XV versus Ulster, 1959

granted them the rare honour of fielding an Ulster XV
against them, which resulted in a victory for the Dukes by
19 points to 5.

Ten members of the Regiment have been awarded
International caps, and no less than twenty-two have represented the Army or Combined Services. In all this galaxy
of rugby talent one name must surely stand out—the in-
comparable W. F. Browne, usually known as 'Horsey', who
was capped no less than twelve times for Ireland between
1925–1928. He has been described as 'the greatest and most
inspiring leader on a rugby field . . . With him there one felt
that all things were possible, however great the odds
against.' The following story is indicative of his great
courage and determination.

> 'At Sandhurst in 1923, owing to a shoulder broken earlier in
> the term, he had to play centre three-quarter in the match
> against "the Shop."* After the game had been in progress for

* The annual match between the Royal Military College,
Sandhurst and the Royal Military Academy, Woolwich ('The
Shop')—since amalgamated—used to be the most important event
in the Sandhurst and Woolwich rugby season.

about ten minutes [he] again dislocated his shoulder and within minutes of this was kicked badly on the head. Any ordinary mortal would have considered that he was beyond taking any further part in the game. Not so "Horsey"; he played on. I, who was playing outside him, could see that he was in considerable pain but such was his will and determination that he managed to score two tries, one in each half, and so win the match for the R.M.C. I have never seen, nor have I ever heard of, a feat of greater courage on the rugby field. In the dressing room after the match "Horsey" had no recollection of the game.'

This story, recounted in *The Iron Duke* by Lieutenant-Colonel Dalrymple, no mean performer himself on the rugby field and in the boxing ring, explains the affection and admiration felt for 'Horsey' Browne, not only in the Dukes, but wherever rugby football was played. 'His feats are fantastic,' writes Dalrymple, 'when one takes into account that he was only 5ft. 8ins. in height—11 odd stone in weight. He had, however, enormous shoulders and a neck, 19½ ins., that might have done justice to any giant of the prehistoric past.' Browne's sadly premature death left behind him a legend of which his Regiment is rightly proud, for he was not only an inspiring leader on the field but also the gayest of companions off it. He died of leukaemia and almost his last request was that his funeral should take place in the morning lest it should interfere with the regimental sports meeting which was due to be held that afternoon. It is indeed right and proper that his memory should continue to be revered in the Dukes, since it is not only on the battle-field that regimental tradition is made.

The standard set by 'Horsey' Browne and his other fine rugby-playing contemporary, 'Bull' Faithfull, was carried on by other fine players like 'Bonzo' Miles, Jack Dalrymple, George Townsend, Joe Annersley, Jimmy Troop, George Laing, Jeff Reynolds, John Harrison and Charlie Grieve. Nor has this remarkable record suffered from the interruption caused by the Second World War. Soon after the war the names of Hardy and Shuttleworth began to appear regularly in Army and International sides, and they were followed by Gilbert-Smith and Campbell-Lammerton. In many ways Campbell-Lammerton's record has been even more notable than 'Horsey' Browne's. Owing to the Korean war he entered first-class rugby rather later than usual, but soon made up for this enforced delay. He has played in five Army Cup finals (winning two of them) and he played for the Army for seven years in succession, captaining the Army in 1964–65–66. He has been capped 23 times for Scotland and captained Scotland in 1966. This brilliant record was crowned in 1966 when he was selected to captain the British Lions for their tour of Australia, New Zealand and Canada. It is indeed a remarkable achievement.

Although the Dukes are rightly proud of their rugby record, it would be a mistake to assume that the Regiment has concentrated on rugby to the exclusion of every other kind of sport. The Athetics team reached the Army Final in 1958–59, while the Dukes have usually fielded a good cricket side. They have always done well at boxing and held their own at Association Football. The Regiment has also made a name for itself in recent years as a first-class shooting regiment, due largely to the enthusiasm of Lieutenant-Colonel (now Brigadier) Bunbury, and there were four members of the Regiment in the Army 100 in 1952.

The Dukes have always been very much a family regiment in which son has followed father for many generations. Families such as the Gores, Danseys, Brays and Wellesleys span many years in the Regiment's history, as do the Wallers and many others. In recent years the two Moran brothers have followed each other as successive commanding officers of the Regiment, and at the moment of writing the 'Army List' shows not less than twelve sons of the Regiment who are carrying on the family tradition. Herein, surely, lies the strength of the British Army's regimental system, so envied by so many other armies, and which we should be foolish indeed to abandon.

'Horsey' Browne

This ends a necessarily abbreviated account of over two and a half centuries' loyal and faithful service to the Crown. Not all the campaigns in which the Regiment has taken part were crowned with victory, and on some of the battlefields on which it has fought the sun went down on defeat; and yet, throughout these long years of service, the Duke of Wellington's Regiment has never lost heart nor failed to do its duty. The Dukes have been as staunch in adversity as they have been magnanimous in victory—as was the great soldier whose title they so proudly bear.

Appendix I

Battle Honours

The Duke of Wellington's Regiment has been awarded 117 battle honours in all, of which those given below are emblazoned on the Colours. The groups of ten each awarded for the Great War and the Second World War are emblazoned on the Queen's Colour. The remaining 21 are emblazoned on the Regimental Colour.

Dettingen	Mysore	Seringapatam
Ally Ghur	Delhi, 1803	Leswarree
Deig	Corunna	Nive
Peninsula	Waterloo	Alma
Inkerman	Sevastopol	Abyssinia
Relief of Kimberley	Paardeberg	South Africa, 1900–1902
Afghanistan, 1919	The Hook, 1953	Korea, 1952–53
Mons	Marne, 1914, '18	Ypres, 1914, '15, '17
Hill 60	Somme, 1916, '18	Arras, 1917, '18
Cambrai, 1917, '18	Lys	Piave
	Landing at Suvla	
Dunkirk, 1940	St Valéry-en-Caux	Fontenay Le Pesnil
North-West Europe, 1940, 1944–45		
	Djebel Bou Aoukaz 1943	Anzio
Monte Ceco	Sittang, 1942	Chindits, 1944
	Burma, 1942–44	

Appendix
II

The Victoria Crosses of the Regiment

Abyssinian Campaign, 1867–68

> No. 3691 Drummer Michael Magner, 33rd Regiment
> No. 949 Private James Bergin, 33rd Regiment

South African War, 1900–02

> No. 2522 Sergeant James Firth, 1st Bn. the Duke of
> Wellington's (West Riding Regiment).

Great War, 1914–18

> 2nd Lieutenant Henry Kelly, 10th Bn. the Duke of
> Wellington's (West Riding Regiment) (T.F.)
> No. 15805 Private Arnold Loosemoore, 8th Bn. the
> Duke of Wellington's (West Riding Regiment) (T.F.)
> No. 24066 Private Arthur Poulter, 1/4th Bn. the Duke of
> Wellington's (West Riding Regiment) (T.F.)
> No. 34506 Private Henry Tandey, DCM, MM, 5th Bn. the
> Duke of Wellington's (West Riding Regiment) (T.F.)
> 2nd Lieutenant James Palmer Huffam, 5th Bn. the Duke
> of Wellington's (West Riding Regiment) (T.F.)

Second World War, 1939–45

> No. 5891907 Private Richard Burton, 1st Bn. the Duke of
> Wellington's Regiment (West Riding)

Appendix
III

The Regimental Marches

On the reorganization of the Army in 1881 each regiment was allotted an official march by the Horse Guards (War Office). '*The Wellesley*' was authorized as the regimental march of the 33rd and 76th. Prior to 1881 marches had not been officially authorized but had been adopted by regiments on account of some action or event—or because the Commanding Officer liked the tune. In some case marches were presented to regiments by eminent persons. Most regiments continue to play tunes with which they have been connected in the past as well as their regimental march, especially if the latter has a short composition so that continual repetition of it becomes tedious. The decision as to what additional tunes are played has in the past been taken at different times by the Colonel of the Regiment, a committee of officers, or the Commanding Officer.

On the amalgamation of the 1st and 2nd Battalions in 1948 the Colonel of the Regiment decided that in addition to the authorized regimental march, '*The Wellesley*', the following should be played as unofficial marches in the order shown:

> '*ILKLA MOOR*'
> '*I'M NINETY-FIVE*'
> '*SCOTLAND THE BRAVE*'

'*The Wellesley*', named after the Duke of Wellington, is a short, stirring march and was discovered among the Duke's papers after his death. The source of the tune is obscure, but the original is believed to be part of a set of Danish quadrilles, the tune being picked up from the French at Waterloo.

The Wellesley

'*Ilkla Moor*', long popular in both battalions, was arranged for band and bugles by the Bandmaster of the 1st Battalion, Mr Seed, in 1948. In addition to being played on Regimental Guest Nights in both battalions, it was used on recruits' passing-out parades, and the Commanding Officer at that time, now Brigadier Webb-Carter, obtained permission from the Colonel of the Regiment to have the march adopted as an extra unofficial march.

'*I'm Ninety-Five*', an old unofficial march of the 33rd, has been used by a number of regiments. In 1881 it became the official march of the Rifle Brigade, the old 95th Foot, and now the 3rd Royal Green Jackets.

'*Scotland the Brave*' was the unofficial march of the 76th and was played on parade before '*The Wellesley*'. The tune was written by J. Ord Hume, who served as a bandsman in the Royal Scots Greys from 1880–87.

TROOPING THE COLOUR

The following marches are played during the ceremony of Trooping the Colours:

Officers and
Warrant Officers: Take Post —'*Destiny*' (33rd slow march)

The Troop: Slow March —'*Destiny*'
'*Logie o' Buchan*' (76th slow march)

Quick March —'*The British Grenadiers*'

Slow March —'*Grenadiers' Slow March*'

March Past:	Slow March —*'Mollendorf'*
	Quick March —*'I'm Ninety-Five'*
	'Scotland the Brave'
	'The Wellesley'

BEATING OF RETREAT

A favourite tune of Lieutenant-Colonel Lloyd, killed in action when commanding the 1st Battalion in South Africa, was *'Cock o' the North.'* After his death it was decided that *'Cock o' the North'* should always be included in the ceremony of Beating of Retreat.

BEATING OF TATTOO

Tattoo is rarely beaten these days, but by long custom the Regiment plays *'Honours of War'* after the National Anthem, a privilege reputedly reserved only for those regiments who were at Waterloo.

REGIMENTAL GUEST NIGHTS

'Rule Britannia' is played after the four regimental marches on Guest Nights in the Officers' Mess. It is not known when and how the custom originated in the 33rd.; it was not played in the 76th.

Appendix
IV

The Honorary Colours

Following the capture of Ally Ghur and Delhi in September, 1803, the Governor-General of India ordered that the 76th Regiment of Foot should be presented with an Honorary Stand of Colours and that these Honorary Colours should be used while the Regiment continued in India and until His Majesty's pleasure be made known. There is no subsequent record of any pleasure being signified and the actual Colours were not in fact presented to the 76th until after the Regiment had returned to England. By this time, by an order dated October 22, 1806 the Regiment was authorized to bear the word HINDOOSTAN on its Colours, and, by a further order dated February 7, 1807, an Elephant.

These devices were incorporated in the Honorary Colours which were presented by the Honourable East India Company, consecrated in Jersey and handed over to the Regiment by Lieutenant-General Don on January 27, 1808, some five years after they had been awarded by the Governor-General in India. The poles were surmounted by spear-heads inscribed:

> '76th Regiment. These Colours were presented to the Regiment by the Chairman and Court of Directors of the Honourable East India Company in testimony of its meritorious services and distinguished bravery in the different actions recorded upon them.'

On the presentation of these Colours, the previously carried Regulation Colours, presented at Cawnpore in 1801 and by now 'reduced to poles by the shot of the enemy,' were handed over to a Major Covell, commanding the Regiment, and no trace of them has ever since been found.

Hugh Greaves, Halifax

Colours of 1st, 2nd and 3rd Battalions, Halifax, 1953

The East India Company Colours were the only Colours carried by the 76th and were treated in all respects as the Regulation Colours at engagements in Spain, Flanders, Southern France and Canada.

In 1828, after the Regiment's return from Canada, the 76th applied for a new Regulation Stand and, a year later, to the East India Company for a replacement of the Colours presented by the Company in 1808. This was agreed to by the Company in a letter dated May 21, 1829. Accordingly, in 1829, the 76th received replacements for the Regulation Colours originally presented in 1801, and in 1830 replacements for the Honorary or East India Company Colours which had been received in 1808. All four Colours were consecrated in 1830 and thenceforward four Colours were carried.

The Regulation Colours were replaced in 1863, and again in 1888. The Honorary Colours were also replaced by the Secretary of State for India in 1888 while the 76th were in Bermuda. There is no record of their having been consecrated but they were certainly trooped and taken into use. In 1901 all four Colours were destroyed by fire in Rangoon. The War Office replaced the Regulation Colours and the India Office replaced the Honorary Colours. All four Colours were consecrated and presented the the normal way at Lichfield in 1906.

The Honorary Colours were replaced in 1969 by regimental subscription at a ceremony in Hong Kong where a new Honorary Stand of Colours was taken into use at a parade of the 1st Battalion, the Duke of Wellington's Regiment. At this parade the spearheads originally borne on the Colours presented in 1808 were transferred to the new Colours by General Sir Robert Bray, Colonel of the Regiment. These Colours are exactly similar to those carried in 1808. They are therefore much bigger than the Regulation Colours since they were designed to be carried in battle. Modern Colours, on the other hand, are solely ceremonial in nature.

General Sir Robert Bray fixing original spearheads to the new set of Honorary Colours, Hong Kong, 1969

The battle honours borne on the Honorary Queen's and Regimental Colours are:

Ally Ghur,	Sept. 4,	1803
Delhi,	Sept. 11,	1803
Agra,	Oct.	1803
Leswarree,	Nov. 1,	1803
Deig,	Dec. 23,	1804
Peninsula		
Mysore		
Nive		
Corunna		

The above honours have the distinction of being borne on both Colours, and, in addition, bear 'Agra,' which is not carried on any other Colour of the Regiment.

Appendix
V

The Record of the Regiment's Territorial Battalions

It is hardly surprising that the writers of regimental histories should concentrate on the record of the regular battalions since these represent the continuity in the existence of a regiment. Although the traditions of the Militiaman, Volunteer, and Territorial can be traced far back in British history—farther back in fact than the traditions of the Regular Army—it is all too easy to forget the part played by the 'part-time' soldier in contributing to, and maintaining, the traditions of a regiment. Certainly, so far as the Duke of Wellington's Regiment is concerned, the part played by its Territorial battalions in the two great wars of this century cannot be overstressed, and it is to them that the Regiment owes many of its battle honours and no less than five of the nine V.C.s awarded to members of the Regiment.

Volunteer forces of one kind or another have existed in Britain ever since the days of the Anglo-Saxon fyrd. They were embodied in times of danger but reverted to their normal occupations as soon as the danger was thought to be over. The Militia, as it came to be known, was particularly active during the period of the Napoleonic wars, since for much of the time there was a danger of invasion. Many of these militiamen were taken into the regular army and fought in Spain and at Waterloo, but the majority of militia units were disbanded after Napoleon's banishment to St Helena. There followed a long period of military doldrums, when the army stagnated, but in 1859 there was another war-scare, again with France, and Volunteer forces were raised. Three of these Volunteer corps were ultimately linked with the Duke of Wellington's Regiment, namely the 4th, 6th, and 9th West Riding of Yorkshire Volunteers, raised in Halifax, Huddersfield, and the Craven Valley respectively. At first these Volunteer units were very much a law unto themselves, reflecting in their dress, drill and training, the whims of their highly individual commanding officers, who were usually leading members of the local community. However, in 1883 a greater measure of uniformity was imposed when the three Corps became respectively the 1st, 2nd, and 3rd Volunteer Battalions of the Duke of Wellington's Regiment. They were technically only liable for home defence, but companies from the Volunteers did in fact serve in South Africa during the Boer War.

In 1908, as a result of the sweeping reorganisation introduced by Haldane as Secretary of State for War, the Volunteers ceased to exist as such and their place was taken by the Territorial Force, intended not only for Home Defence but also to provide the second line for the Regular Army in the event of a major war. A consequence of the 1908 reorganization was that the three Volunteer battalions of the Regiment became four Territorial battalions—4th, 5th, 6th and 7th Battalions, the Duke of Wellington's Regiment (T.F.). It required special legislation before the Territorials could be sent overseas but there can be no doubt that Haldane's scheme was a far-seeing and sensible one; the pity of it is that Kitchener, when he became Secretary of State for War in 1914, lacked knowledge of the Territorial Force and failed to make full use of it for the vast expansion that was needed. He virtually ignored the Territorials and raised 'New Army' battalions instead.

In April, 1915 the 1/4th, 1/5th, 1/6th and 1/7th now described as first line Territorial battalions, went overseas as the 147th Brigade of the 49th (West Riding) Division. They were to see their share of fighting in the bloody shambles of France and Flanders and were soon to show that the Territorial soldier, when properly trained and led, had nothing to fear by comparison with the Regular. The 2/4th, 2/5th, 2/6th and 2/7th Battalions went to France in January, 1917 in the 186th Brigade of the 62nd (West Riding) Division and they, too, were to distinguish themselves. The 3/4th, 3/5th, 3/6th, and 3/7th Battalions were retained at home throughout the war and were employed in the training and drafting of reinforcements for the battalions overseas. In addition six 'Service' battalions were raised— 8th, 9th, 10th, 11th, 12th, and 13th. The 8th fought at Gallipoli, in Egypt, and in France; the 9th fought in France, and the 10th in France and Italy. The 11th did not go overseas, the 12th was turned into a Labour, or Pioneer battalion in France, while the 13th was a Garrison battalion for much of its existence. It did, however, get to France in July, 1918, by which time it had ceased to be a Garrison battalion, and it participated in the general advance as part of 178th Brigade. It was in the front line on Armistice Day and ended its days at Dunkirk, where it functioned as a demobilization camp until November, 1919.

The four Territorial battalions with which the Regiment had begun the war had increased to twelve by the end of the war, and six Service battalions had also been raised. No leas than 21 battle honours were gained for the Regiment by these battalions, including the three Colour honours of 'Cambrai, 1917', 'Landing at Suvla', and 'Piave'. This was a proud record which the then Colonel of the Regiment, Lieutenant-General Sir Herbert Belfield, saw fit to single out for special mention when the history of the Regiment during the Great War was published in 1927.

By then, however, the Territorials had undergone another reorganization. In this connection it may be pertinent to comment that the history of the British Army between major wars has been remarkably consistent; it has either been allowed to stagnate, far from the public gaze, or it has been subjected to continuous and intensive reorganization. The happy medium, so long claimed as being a peculiar virtue of the British people, has never been allowed to apply so far as the Army is concerned. In the 1921 reorganization the title of the Territorial Force was changed to the Territorial Army, but there was no change in the titles of the four Territorial battalions of the Dukes. They suffered, of course, from the continual search for economy, their equipment becoming increasingly obsolete, and it was only their enthusiasm which kept the battalions in being. Nevertheless, during those difficult years from 1920 to 1935, one great benefit did accrue to the Regiment, and that was the close touch it was able to maintain, through its Territorial battalions, with the people of the West Riding of Yorkshire; and if there is anything to be said for the territorial connection, which I firmly believe to be of incalculable value, it is to be found here in the link provided for the Regiment with the people of Halifax, Huddersfield, Skipton, and Milnsbridge, by its Territorial battalions.

It was becoming clear from 1935 onwards that a war with Germany might well be forced on us, and for those responsible for the fashioning of Britain's defence policy, it became distressingly obvious that the years which the locusts had eaten were going to exact a severe penalty. Air defence, for example, was virtually non-existent and in 1936 the 5th Battalion became a Searchlight Regiment as the 43rd (5th Duke of Wellington's Regiment) Anti-Aircraft Battalion, R.E. (T.A.). This was only the first of its bewildering changes of title; in 1944 it became the 43rd Garrison Regiment, R.A. (5th D.W.R.), and the following year it changed to 600th Regiment (5th D.W.R.) R.A. However it did throughout retain its connection with Air defence. Changes of title are, of course, easier to arrange than the provision of modern equipment but as the threat of Hitler's Panzers grew more obvious, belated attention was paid to the requirement of anti-tank defence. The 4th Battalion

Central Office of Information

Recruits at the Depot, 1952

became the 58th Anti-Tank Regiment (D.W.R.) R.A., and when all Territorial battalions were required to form second battalions in 1938, the 2/4th Battalion became the 68th Anti-Tank Regiment, R.A. The 6th and 7th Battalions were also required to form second battalions in the 1938 expansion. This looked well enough on paper, but in reality meant nothing since there was insufficient equipment to bring even the first line battalions up to a reasonable scale.

During the Second World War, as in the Great War, all the Territorial battalions of the Regiment greatly distinguished themselves in the various theatres in which they were employed. They made a tremendous contribution to the Regiment's traditions. It would take too long to describe in any detail the exploits of those wearing the Dukes' cap-badge who fought as Infantry, Gunners, and Royal Armoured Corps, or played their part in the vital task of training reinforcements in the United Kingdom. Territorial soldiers of the Dukes fought in France, the Low Countries, Germany, North Africa, Burma, Italy, Greece, Java, and in the air defence of this country. They garrisoned Iceland, helped to liberate Holland, and found themselves involved in the bewildering political situation in Sumatra during the aftermath of Japan's defeat. They proved, if proof be needed, the enduring qualities of Britain's citizen soldiers, and made a splendid and lasting contribution to the traditions of the Duke of Wellington's Regiment.

Inevitably, victory was followed by yet another reorganization. The outcome of this, in 1947, was the retention of only one infantry battalion, the 7th; the others became the 382nd Medium Regiment R.A. (D.W.R.) T.A., 578th (5/D.W.R.) Heavy Anti-Aircraft Regiment R.A. T.A., and 673rd Light Anti-Aircraft Regiment R.A. (D.W.R.) T.A. Despite these tongue-twisting titles, and quite different roles and equipment, the long-established loyalties remained unaffected; 'once a Duke, always a Duke', they said in the West Riding. Hardly had the dust been allowed to settle on the post-war reorganization than another change took place. Anti-Aircraft Command followed the longbow into history and the three Artillery regiments who traced their origins to the 4th, 5th and 6th Battalions of the Dukes became 'P', 'Q', and 'R' Batteries of 382nd Medium Regiment R.A. (D.W.R.) T.A. This was in 1955, but if anyone thought that reorganization had run its course they were soon to be disillusioned. Two years later the old 5th and 7th Battalions were amalgamated to form the 5th/7th Battalion the Duke of Wellington's Regiment T.A., and there was then a pause for breath.

The search for economies in the defence budget resulted in another reorganization towards the end of 1960. The 5th/7th Battalion was amalgamated with 382nd Medium Regiment R.A. to produce the West Riding Battalion (the Duke of Wellington's Regiment) T.A., with its headquarters in Huddersfield; companies and detachments were spread right across the West Riding in Huddersfield, Halifax, Mirfield, Skipton, Keighley, Mossley, and Thongsbridge. After many years of change the old 4th, 5th, 6th and 7th Battalions had returned to their original role as infantry, but this time as companies and platoons, and no longer as battalions. Although many a good Gunner must have sighed, the Dukes were glad to be back in their traditional role as the infantrymen of the West Riding of Yorkshire.

But if any of them thought that this would be the end of reorganization, they were soon to discover how wrong they were. The changing nature of this country's defence requirements, coupled with the overriding requirement to save money, led in 1967 to the most drastic reorganization since Haldane organized the Territorial Force in 1908. After a searching, and often bitter debate, the Territorial Army virtually ceased to exist. A new Reserve organization was introduced known as the Territorial and Army Volunteer Reserve (T. & A.V.R.), divided into three categories, and specifically intended to reinforce the Regular Army, either collectively or as individuals, in an emergency. The old concept of the Territorial Army as the second line of the Regular Army, with its own Divisions and Brigades, was swept away, and a much smaller force, which was intended to be better trained and better equipped, was substituted.

As far as the Duke of Wellington's Regiment was concerned the 1967 reorganization involved the disappearance of its sole remaining Territorial battalion. In its place was formed the Yorkshire Volunteers (T. & A.V.R. II) with an overseas commitment in the event of emergency or war. The four Yorkshire infantry regiments (including the since disbanded York & Lancaster Regiment) each provide one company, which in the case of the Duke of Wellington's Regiment is C Company based in Halifax. There was also formed the West Riding Territorials (T. & A.V.R. III) with a Home Guard role in the event of general war, but in less than two years the West Riding Territorials were abolished. They were replaced in 1969 by the West Riding Battalion (D.W.R.) (Cadre) consisting of 3 officers and 5 other ranks with the task of supporting the Volunteer Company in case of emergency, providing a base for expansion should the need arise, and keeping alive the traditions of the 4th, 5th, 6th and 7th Battalions. It was also charged with the responsibility of keeping contact with former members— a diminishing task as former members grow older and memories of the old T.A. grow dimmer and dimmer. The various categories of the T. & A.V.R., as introduced in 1967, have now ceased to exist and there remains only T. & A.V.R.

It will be seen from this short summary that the 'part-time' members of the Dukes have played a most important part in the life of the Regiment ever since the first Volunteer battalions were raised in 1859. They have been reorganized time after time but have never allowed this to affect their enthusiasm nor their determination to maintain the great traditions of *their* Regiment. They have added lustre to the Regiment's name by their gallantry in war, and in times of peace they have kept alive the volunteer principle, often at great expense to their personal life and to their pockets. But above all, and perhaps most importantly, they have provided a vital link between the Regulars, so often overseas, and the people of the West Riding, and by their presence in the midst of the civilian community have served to remind their fellow-citizens of the Army's existence.